GREAT AMERICANS IN SPORTS

BLAKE GRIFFIN

MATT CHRISTOPHER

Little, Brown and Company

New York Boston

Little, Brown and Company

Hachette Book Group
1290 Avenue of the Americas, New York, NY 10104
Visit us at lb-kids.com

mattchristopher.com

Little, Brown and Company is a division of Hachette Book Group, Inc.
The Little, Brown name and logo are trademarks of Hachette Book Group, Inc.

The publisher is not responsible for websites (or their content) that are not owned by the publisher.

First Edition: December 2015

Matt Christopher® is a registered trademark of Matt Christopher Royalties, Inc.

Written by Zachary Rau

Cover illustration by Michael Cho

Library of Congress Cataloging-in-Publication Data

Rau, Zachary.
Great Americans in sports, Blake Griffin / [written by Zachary Rau] — First Edition.
pages cm
"Matt Christopher."
ISBN 978-0-316-29663-2 (trade pbk.) — ISBN 978-0-316-29664-9 (ebook) — ISBN 978-0-316-29662-5 (library edition ebook) 1. Griffin, Blake, 1989— Juvenile literature. 2. Basketball players—United States—Biography— Juvenile literature. I. Title.
GV884.G76R38 2015
796.323092—dc23
[B]
2015025219

10 9 8 7 6 5 4 3 2 1

RRD-C

Printed in the United States of America

CONTENTS

INTRODUCTION 1

CHAPTER ONE: 1989–2001 3
Growing Up in Oklahoma City

CHAPTER TWO: 2002–2005 10
Back-to-Back Brothers

CHAPTER THREE: 2005–2006 21
Stepping Out of the Shadow

CHAPTER FOUR: 2006–2007 28
Making History

CHAPTER FIVE: 2007–2008 34
Family Reunion

CHAPTER SIX: 2008–2009 56
The Griffin Brothers' Last Stand

CHAPTER SEVEN: 2009 72
March Madness

CHAPTER EIGHT: 2009–2010 82
NBA: Year One

CHAPTER NINE: 2010–2011 90
The Rookie Season Do-Over

CHAPTER TEN: 2011–2012 98
The Lockout Season

CHAPTER ELEVEN: 2012–2013   112
Building a Champion Is Never Easy

CHAPTER TWELVE: 2013–2014   120
The Next Level

CHAPTER THIRTEEN: 2014 AND BEYOND   144
The Dawn of a New Era

INFOGRAPHICS   149

INTRODUCTION

It's difficult to tell how tall basketball players are from watching a televised game. When they're standing and playing next to each other, everyone on the court looks to be of normal height and weight. It isn't until the postgame interviews, when the players stand next to reporters, that it becomes clear that most NBA players tower above the rest of us like giants.

And it's no wonder: the average height of an NBA player is ten inches taller than that of the average American man, while the average weight of an NBA player is sixty pounds greater. These aren't statistics that are trending upward as the game becomes more modern—they have remained relatively consistent since 1980. Which is all to say that to be a contender in the NBA, it helps to be tall.

Even in this land of giants, Blake Griffin stands out. At six feet ten inches tall and with an incredibly powerful physique, he could easily be mistaken for a football player rather than an NBA All-Star. With one of the highest vertical jumps in the league,

Blake's jump is even more impressive than his height. He has been winning slam-dunk contests since he was in high school.

Blake sees the floor like a guard and has become the most exciting young player in the NBA. Though everyone talks about his physical abilities, it is clear that his work ethic is what drives him to get better every year. Blake's work ethic is something he learned from his family as he grew up in Oklahoma.

CHAPTER ONE
1989–2001

GROWING UP IN OKLAHOMA CITY

Looking at Blake Griffin now, he is hard to imagine as a child, because his size and stature make him seem larger than life. But before he was "Blake Griffin, NBA star," he was "Little Griffin"—a skinny boy who just wanted to play.

Blake Austin Griffin was born to Gail and Tommy Griffin on March 16, 1989. Tommy was a successful high school basketball coach in Oklahoma City, Oklahoma. Blake's older brother, Taylor, was born three years earlier and had been eagerly waiting for his baby brother's arrival. From the day that Blake was born, he and Taylor were each other's biggest fans.

Like many brothers, Taylor and Blake were best friends—as well as rivals. Both boys were home-schooled by their mother until they were teenagers. So instead of getting time apart in different school classrooms during the day, they spent every minute together. That time together bred rivalry. Every game of H.O.R.S.E. and every board game played brought out the fierce competitive nature of the Griffin boys. They could turn just about anything into a contest!

When Taylor started playing T-ball, Blake immediately wanted to play, too. Tommy could tell both of his boys were talented, but he noticed something else in his younger son: because Blake was always three years behind Taylor in terms of skill and athleticism, Blake had to work harder and learn to be tougher so that he could keep up.

"Taylor was playing T-ball, and Blake was four years old. We were winning, so Blake got a chance to hit the ball," Tommy remembered. "The first time he hit it, he had a double; the second time, he had a triple. Every time he hit it, it went to the fence. He was only four. We started thinking, 'Huh, maybe there's a future there.'"

Though they were homeschooled, Taylor and Blake were able to join many other social activities. Both showed a natural athletic ability at an early age, and they played on a variety of sports teams, including baseball, basketball, football, and soccer. The Griffins believed in letting their boys have a childhood at every possible opportunity, rather than forcing them to take sports too seriously. Tommy was careful not to push them toward a specific sport or to expect them to practice like they were players on his own high school basketball team. But being the sons of Tommy Griffin meant Blake and Taylor were around winning basketball teams their entire lives, and both boys picked up much of their work ethic from their father.

Tommy was still a child when he learned many of the hard lessons he would later teach his athletes, students, and sons. When he was ten years old, his father, Big Tommy Griffin, passed away, leaving his mother to raise Tommy, her only child, as a single parent. His entire neighborhood helped out by watching young Tommy. If he ever did anything wrong, his neighbors would say, "Hey, Little Griffin, you don't need to do that." Tommy's neighborhood was more of a family, and his mother was always there for him, too.

Still, life was sometimes tough for Tommy, and he looked toward role models outside of his household. One of those role models was his swimming coach, Roger Pierce. One day Tommy would be a great athlete, but he encountered his share of rejection early on. In eighth grade, Tommy was cut from the basketball team and was very disappointed. Coach Pierce suggested that he try swimming instead. Tommy had never considered swimming, but Coach

Pierce promised to teach him. Three years later, Tommy was swimming at an all-American level.

Being cut from the basketball team had taught Tommy an important lesson about perseverance: when one door closes, another opens. If he hadn't been cut from the basketball team, he might never have tried swimming, and never would have had the opportunity to swim at such a high level.

After playing football and basketball at Northern Oklahoma Junior College, Tommy was a two-sport star at Northwestern Oklahoma State University in basketball and track. He graduated in 1970 with a degree in health and physical education, and he took his first job out of school as an assistant coach of the boy's basketball team at Classen High School. Tommy took over the head coaching position four years later, staying fifteen years at Classen.

Tommy won two state championships with Classen: one in 1975 and another in 1980. Unfortunately, the high school closed in 1985, leaving him without a job. The two championships looked great on his résumé, but a job as a varsity head coach is hard to find, so he swallowed his pride and took an assistant position at the school he once attended, Douglass High School.

Tommy decided he was going to do whatever it

took to become a head coach again, even if that meant starting over at the bottom of the ladder. The Griffin family didn't see adversity as an obstacle; they saw it as an opportunity. Tommy's work ethic would later become a cornerstone of Blake's and Taylor's lives; if their father would willingly do whatever it took to get the job done, then they would do whatever it took as well.

Gail and Tommy had met while working at Classen High School in the early 1980s, at a time when interracial marriages were still frowned upon in some places. Luckily for Afro-Haitian Tommy and Caucasian Gail, Classen was a very diverse school, and no one paid their relationship much attention. Periodically, the two would get strange looks, but Tommy and Gail learned to ignore these negative reactions. Looking past the color of people's skin, and not letting skin color define how they thought of themselves or others, were important values that Tommy and Gail would instill in their children.

While Tommy spent his days teaching and coaching, Gail was in charge of homeschooling Taylor and Blake. The choice to homeschool the boys hadn't come lightly. When Taylor first went off to kindergarten, Gail realized that, as a former teacher, she wanted to have a bigger role in the education of her sons. She wanted to prepare Blake and Taylor to succeed academically, and also to be good people. The Griffins taught the boys the importance of treating others the way they would like to be treated. The family gave when they could and helped others as often as possible. Sometimes that meant volunteering. Other times it meant helping out a family with a meal. The Griffins didn't have much, but what they had, they shared.

Tommy left his assistant job at Douglass when his first boss from Classen High, Coach Charles Davis, called with a unique opportunity. Davis was the head coach at John Marshall High School, and he was strongly considering retirement. He asked Tommy if he'd like to come to John Marshall as an assistant and take over once Davis retired. Tommy accepted and took over the head coaching position after only one year. He stayed at John Marshall for twelve years and coached teams to two more Oklahoma State Championships, in 1996 and 2000.

The John Marshall basketball teams made a big impression on Blake and Taylor. The teams became examples of what it took to win a championship and would act as a blueprint for the Griffin brothers' successes later in life. Watching the John Marshall basketball team, Blake decided that he wanted to win every championship he could.

Tommy spent years helping to shape the John Marshall students into young men—both on the court and in the classroom—so it is no wonder that he and Gail raised two amazing young men of their own. Even before their four magical seasons at Oklahoma Christian School, everyone knew that with their physical strength, strong characters, and determination, Blake and Taylor were going to be something very special.

CHAPTER TWO
2002–2005

BACK-TO-BACK BROTHERS

After Tommy guided John Marshall to a 2000 Oklahoma State Championship, and despite having a great team in 2001, he decided to leave Marshall to take an assistant coach position at Oklahoma Christian School. Both of his sons were planning on starting school at OCS, and Tommy wanted to be closer to them. As successful as he had been at John Marshall, Tommy didn't like that his schedule there kept him from cheering for Taylor and Blake at their games.

"He loves coaching," said Gail Griffin, "but the thing that kills him now is missing our sons' events." Tommy's priority was his family, and he was happy to make the move.

By the time Blake started classes at OCS as an eighth grader and Taylor was a high school sophomore, Tommy had already been promoted to head coach of the varsity boy's basketball team. This made for an easier transition from homeschooling for the young Griffins. While they wouldn't see their mother during the school day, as they had for most of their lives, they would get to see their father.

Blake started his freshman year at OCS in the shadow of his older brother. Taylor was a junior now, and a clear choice for starter on the basketball team, while Blake was still being called Little Griffin. Though Blake wasn't actually *little*, he hadn't hit his final growth spurt or filled out yet, either. He was at the awkward stage when teenagers' bodies grow at different rates and they have to adjust to being taller and bigger.

The younger Griffin had always chased after his older brother, trying to keep up with Taylor and his friends, but typically losing to Taylor at everything. Those experiences lit a competitive fire inside Blake. Now that both brothers were in high school and on the same team, Blake could focus all his competitive energy on his opponents rather than on his brother.

"They were really competitive and very physical in driveway basketball games. Blake was always the kind that hates to lose," Tommy said. "Once they became teammates, they were still competitive, but it wasn't Blake versus Taylor. It was 'us versus them.' Now they are best friends. Even when Taylor was on the East Coast and Blake was on the West Coast, they still talked every day."

Perhaps the greatest advantage to playing those countless games in the driveway against each other was this: Blake and Taylor knew each other's tendencies on the court. They knew when the other liked to pass the ball, when a pump fake meant a shot was coming, and when to expect a drive and dish. The brothers had played so many games against each other that they had practically developed a nonverbal language—one that only the two of them could understand. Though this language originated when they were opponents, in the end, it helped them become better teammates.

The brothers' first year playing together was a great season for the Oklahoma Christian Saints. The team went undefeated, winning an Oklahoma State Championship when they beat Riverside for the 3A title. Blake was still very young, playing mostly off the bench, while his brother and the Saints' leading scorer, Joel Evans, were the stars of the team. Blake made the most of his limited minutes, studying his brother's game from the bench. He watched how Taylor rebounded and boxed out, how Evans drove the lane or dropped to shoot, and more. When

Blake got into the game, he did his best to imitate the older players. He wanted to get better, but he also wanted to help the team win, so he waited for his chance to shine.

Going into the 2004 championship game, Oklahoma Christian had won most of their regular season games easily, and the team's big win gave Coach Griffin his fifth state championship. Blake, who was nicknamed Tayshaun Prince because he was as skinny as the NBA star, was still adjusting to the style of play at the high school level. He went two-for-two for four points and two personal fouls in the championship game.

Taylor, on the other hand, had a stellar game. He was a vacuum around the hoop, pulling down fifteen of the Saints' twenty-one rebounds. Taylor had averaged a double-double for the season, and he backed it up in the championship game, scoring seventeen points while going six-for-twelve in a competition that saw the lead change hands five times during the first half.

Over the course of the three games of the 2004 Boys 3A State Tournament, Taylor Griffin had scored sixty-three points and grabbed thirty-six rebounds, ultimately earning the tournament MVP. And through it all, Blake was watching—and learning.

Nothing was going to be easy during Blake's second season. As the reigning 3A champs and the unanimous preseason first-ranked 3A team in the state, there was a lot of pressure on the Saints. Every team in Oklahoma was gunning for them, and they would be facing tough opponents, so the Saints players knew that they would have to play even better than the year before if they were to repeat as champions. Taylor, who had committed to playing college ball at the University of Oklahoma, and Blake would have to play the best basketball of their lives.

"I want to end with a title," said Taylor. "I'm excited about going to OU, but I really want to win this year."

Blake was on board with that plan, praising Taylor's leadership and saying, "Taylor's in command, and if I can do what he does, that would be great."

To help make Taylor's dream a reality, Blake had worked on his post and defensive games in the summer leading up to the 2004–2005 season. By the start of his sophomore season, Blake had earned a starting role on the Saints varsity squad, right next to his brother. For the first time in their lives, the Griffin brothers would be starting in the same frontcourt. Blake was still an inch shorter than his brother that year, measuring in at six feet five inches, but he had put on some weight and was starting to fill out his frame. The brothers were a brutal interior defensive unit, a matchup that no coach could game-plan for. Further helping the team's chances, Oklahoma Christian had four players who were taller than six feet on the court for most of the game. That made the Saints one of the biggest teams in the state, and easily the biggest in Class 3A.

This season was something Coach Griffin would cherish for the rest of his life. He got to watch both of his boys on the court at the same time, defending the state title. The pressure that came with it was nothing compared to the pride Tommy felt when he watched his sons play together.

The season did not start the way Oklahoma Christian had expected. An early loss to Sequoyah High School in December shocked the Saints and forced them to reevaluate their identity. It was clear that the Saints hadn't yet figured out how to pull out a tight game and that they were a very different group from the previous season's undefeated team. With only two seniors on the whole squad, this team was unusually young, so Coach Griffin decided that he had to keep some older players on the court at all times to provide much-needed leadership.

That early loss pushed OCS out of the top spot in the rankings. The Saints started to play even more competitively to get back to number one. Blake and Taylor bodied up anyone willing to risk driving on them. They battled for every rebound. They dove for every loose ball. They put the Griffin stamp on every game. In an early February matchup, Blake scored twenty-one points, and Taylor put up nineteen to score over half of the team's total points on the way to a 73–30 win.

From that game on, it was clear to everyone watching that, though this was Taylor's team for the rest of this season, Blake was showing signs of becoming something really special. When Blake found his rhythm, he was impossible to guard.

Going into the first round of the 3A State Tournament, the Saints were ranked second, behind only one team: Sequoyah. Repeating as the state champions was a real possibility, especially after the Saints won clear victories of 71–45 and 49–29 in their two semifinal games. They were on their way to the state final!

The state championship was an emotional game

for the Griffin family. They knew that it would be the last time Tommy would get to coach his sons together and that it might be Blake and Taylor's last chance to play together, too. Taylor would be headed to Norman, Oklahoma, the following year to play for the University of Oklahoma, and no one knew where Blake would go to college, since he still had two years of high school left to finish.

The game was the matchup that everyone, especially Blake and Taylor, had hoped for: the top-ranked Sequoyah High School against Oklahoma Christian School, the second-ranked team in Class 3A. The Saints and the Griffins would get a chance to make up for their first loss of the season—and to become repeat state champs.

To win the game, the Griffin boys knew they would need to control the paint, and Blake and Taylor dictated the game's tone from the opening whistle. Oklahoma Christian challenged every possession, pressing the faster and more athletic Sequoyah. On offense, the Saints worked their half-court sets to find the open man outside against Sequoyah's zone defense.

With the Sequoyah team focused on limiting Taylor's touches, Oklahoma Christian staked an early lead behind three three-pointers from Tyler Phillips. The Sequoyah team answered back as their sharp-shooting guard hit a pair of threes, pulling the game to within three points. Taylor hit two free throws, and Blake added a conventional three-point play, ending the first quarter with an eight-point Saints lead. The Saints defense then limited Sequoyah to a measly five points in the second quarter. At half, the Saints held a comfortable 31–17 lead.

The Saints came out of the half with a fourteen-point lead and a fire in their eyes. The second-half game plan was the same as the first: Coach Griffin wanted to see the Saints take control of the game from the tip-off, so the Saints pressured the ball and stifled Sequoyah's normally hot outside shooting. The Saints out-rebounded Sequoyah by a final margin of thirty to ten. They shot 58 percent from the field and hit eleven of fifteen free throws. Blake had a game high of nine rebounds, while Taylor added six of his own. Together, the brothers tallied half of the Saints' total rebounds. There were no second chances when Sequoyah missed a shot, because one of the Griffins already had the ball.

Toward the beginning of the fourth quarter, something special happened: Taylor racked two monstrous, backboard-shaking dunks that blew the lid off the Saints fans. Just minutes later, Blake responded with two of his own dunks, ending any possible comeback for Sequoyah. It was as if Taylor was passing the torch to Blake—and Blake was ready to lead. With the game in hand, Taylor walked off the court for the last time as a Saint to a standing ovation. He hugged his father, grabbed a towel, and sat on the bench, remembering all the good times he'd had playing Saints basketball.

"Coming off the court for the last time is something I'll never forget," said Taylor. "Winning the gold ball with my father, brother, and teammates in my last game in high school—the feelings are really indescribable."

At the end of it all, Blake and Taylor had been an impossible matchup for Sequoyah. The two towering brothers dominated on both sides of the court in their last high school game together. Taylor dropped a game-high nineteen points, on seven-of-ten shooting, to go with his three blocked shots and six rebounds. Blake, the second highest scorer in the game, added twelve points to the tally.

Taylor was named the tournament MVP again and was a member of that year's Oklahoman Super 5 team, which is made up of the five best players at their positions in the state. Blake wasn't overlooked that year, as he was named to the Oklahoma Little All-City and All-State teams and a member of the all-tourney team. Back-to-back state championships for OCS brought Coach Griffin's state championship total to six—but this last one, with both of his boys starting, was extra special. It was a great season for the Griffins.

CHAPTER THREE
2005–2006

STEPPING OUT OF THE SHADOW

Blake played in Amateur Athletic Union (AAU) basketball tournaments all across the country over the summer on Oklahoma's Athletes First team. It helped him keep his mind off his brother leaving home soon for the first time.

One of Blake's teammates that year was Sam Bradford, who would later be picked first overall in the 2010 NFL draft. When Blake wasn't on the court, he spent time in the gym that the Bradfords owned. He had spent his first two years of high school trying to put on weight, and he had some success, but it wasn't until that off-season that he started to see real results. When the season started, Blake was much bigger and stronger.

As Blake entered his junior year at OCS, the pressure of a three-peat sat on his shoulders. Up until that year, Blake always had his brother's lead to follow. With Taylor away at college, Blake would have to play as well as Taylor had the past two seasons—or even better.

OCS returned four seniors that season, led by the outstanding Tyler Phillips, who brought a wealth of experience and composure to the team. The upperclassmen were the backbone of the team that year. Even so, Blake missed his older brother on and off the basketball court. The whole family did.

The Saints ran into some unexpected trouble early in the season, when they lost their second game. That taste of losing, no matter how brief, shook the team's confidence and lit a fire under them.

Over the course of the next ten games of the regular season, the Saints beat their opponents by an average of 37 points. The team would go on to win every matchup after their second-game loss, including a three-point win over the eventual Class 4A state champs.

During the state tournament, Blake's game took another step forward. He solidified his place in OCS history, and as one of the state's best players, with a series of phenomenal performances.

In the state quarterfinals, Blake and the Saints

won by twenty-four points. Blake finished the game with twenty-eight of his points on the scoreboard.

In the semifinals, the Oktaha High School Tigers had seen how Blake was playing and had hoped they could somehow stop the six-foot-eight-inch junior from OCS. Every time the Tigers dropped a defender into the paint, it opened up the outside shooting lanes for senior Tyler Phillips, who hit six out of eight from behind the arc, ending the game with twenty-four points. When the Tigers shifted their defense and pressed outside, it left Blake open underneath. With space, Blake could find his way to the basket—and to thirteen rebounds and twenty-two points. The Saints scored more points in the second half alone than their opponents scored in the entire game. They were one step closer to their three-peat.

In the state finals, the Saints faced the same Washington High School team that they had beaten in the regional finals, who had gone on quite a run to secure the school's first berth to the finals. But no matter how successful the Warriors had been in their playoff run, they were no match for OCS and for Blake, whose play got stronger every quarter.

The final score does not tell the real tale of that game. At half, the Saints led 37–14. By the time the score hit 55–21, with three minutes left in the game, Coach Griffin pulled his starters to give the bench players championship court time. Washington had managed to gain only seven points through the third and most of the fourth quarters. With the Saints starters out, Washington was able to find some success on the offensive side of the ball, and the score ended up being 57–40. It was still a clear win for the Saints, but the game was much closer than it could have been.

"We're not finished," Blake said after winning his third golden ball. "We have a great tradition and we want to build a dynasty here at OCS."

Blake was named the Player of the Year after that season, and was selected as a member of the Oklahoman Super 5 team and the Little All-City Boys Basketball starting five. But the best part was being able to show Taylor his third trophy.

Blake had grown so much that season. Stepping out of Taylor's shadow, he had begun to find his own identity as a player and a leader—and he still had a year of school left to make a mark. Not many players in the country were four-peat state champions, but it looked like something Blake had set his sights on.

Within a month of winning his third golden ball at the state tournament, many big-name schools that had been lightly recruiting Blake began to make late bids to sign the now six-foot-ten-inch power forward. The University of North Carolina, Connecticut, Texas, Kansas, and Coach K—Mike Krzyzewski—at Duke all pushed hard to land Blake.

But the best recruiter was Taylor Griffin. Blake was already playing pickup with Taylor and other players at Oklahoma, and was getting comfortable there. Taylor was selling Blake on the idea of attending the University of Oklahoma to play under the new head coach, Jeff Capel.

Coach Capel had played college ball at Duke under Coach K and played pro ball in Europe and Canada before serving as an assistant on his father's staff at Old Dominion University. He was a rising star in the college basketball world, known for having been one of the youngest Division I head coaches ever when Virginia Commonwealth University made him head coach in 2002. He was a major steal for the University of Oklahoma when the school brought him over to helm the Sooners basketball program, but he had a lot of work to do. Landing one of the nation's best players and one of the best in-state prospects would be another steal for the program, and would help to announce Capel's arrival as a force in the Big 12 Conference.

Taylor wanted his brother on the team and pitched Blake at the dinner table when he came home on the weekends. "Taylor is such a good salesperson," Tommy Griffin said when asked about Taylor's role in recruiting Blake. "He sold him on OU."

On top of that, the spotlight and all the calls and texts were a lot for Blake to handle. He wanted the whole process to be finished so that he could concentrate on playing ball. Blake had set his top choices early (Kansas, Duke, Florida, Texas, and Michigan State all made it onto the list), but ultimately, the chance to play two more seasons with his big brother was just too good to pass up. His mom and dad could come see him play if he attended Oklahoma, and he could go home for the weekends. Best of all, Blake and Taylor could rule the Big 12 together.

"Whenever you can, play in your home state," Blake said at the time about his decision. "And play in front of the people you grew up with—all your friends and family can come see you play. It's a big deal to me." In the end, the most important thing to Blake was always family.

Blake committed to being a Sooner on May 14, 2006. It was a huge victory for Capel. He had kept Oklahoma's best player in state, and he had managed to fortify his frontcourt. Now he would have the two Griffin brothers to protect the basket and to anchor his defense. Coach Capel could see, even then, that Blake would be special. But he wasn't sure if the young man was strong enough to become truly great. Coach Capel would have to be hard on Blake to make him into the best player he could be.

Once Blake expressed his intentions, the phone calls and texts from coaches began to slow and eventually stopped. That allowed Blake to focus on summer ball and his senior season. He could also focus on hitting the weights in order to get even bigger and stronger.

CHAPTER FOUR
2006–2007

MAKING HISTORY

By the time the school year started, the whole state expected the Saints to win another title. Blake was one of the top twenty players in the country, and he was a senior. It seemed a championship win was destined—four state titles in a row would be historic for the school, for Coach Griffin, and for Blake. Everyone just wanted to skip the season to get right to the championship game.

But every game has to be played, and every win must be earned. It would take multiple wins for the Saints to actually secure the championship, and winning is hard work.

The Saints started the season in fine form. They won their early games easily, despite some less-than-perfect performances—but a trend began to emerge that would follow Blake for the rest of his career. With no answer for Blake's physical abilities, many rival teams resorted to hacking the young power forward. Some teams used their biggest players to foul him as hard as they could. Other teams used their tiny guards to draw fouls by pushing him when he was shooting. Everyone wanted to make it difficult for Blake to play the game.

In early December, it became clear that these tactics might actually cost the Saints some wins. For example, in a game against the talented Verdigris Cardinals, Blake had a hard time adjusting to the Verdigris defensive scheme. The Cardinals bumped, pushed, and, in general, fouled Blake whenever he got the ball. Because Blake was so much bigger than the guard, referees wouldn't call the fouls. It was a frustrating game, and the Saints ended up losing, 53–48. That game showed how difficult it would be for Blake to get a call, since— unless the foul was blatant—referees were going to give the Saints' opponents the benefit of the doubt. It was also a good indicator of how far teams were willing to go to win against Oklahoma Christian.

Just a few weeks later, Coach Griffin tested the Saints with new teams—teams that were better than Oklahoma Christian. The Saints took a trip to New York to compete in a holiday basketball tournament, where they played the toughest team they would face all season. They ended up losing that game, but it wasn't a complete wipeout. The fact that they could hold their own against such a talented team helped the Saints realize that they could play with the very best. Thanks to Coach Griffin's test, the Saints really believed in themselves. They stormed into the state tournament as a team on a mission: to win their fourth state title.

The Saints had the biggest starting lineup in the 2A class. In their first tournament game, Blake put up twenty-three points on the way to a convincing victory. The Saints were ahead by so many points that Blake was rested for much of the second half.

In the semifinals, the Saints played tenth-ranked Foyil, and Blake backed up all of the hype that surrounded him. With a slow and steady pace, he and the Saints built a lead that was simply too great for the Panthers to overcome. Blake scored thirty-four points, blocked six shots, grabbed eleven rebounds, and left the game with over three minutes on the clock and a thirty-two-point lead. Foyil was a very good team that year, but the Saints were just that much better.

In the other semifinal, the Pawnee Black Bears

and their star player, Keiton Page, put up 111 points on Oktaha High School. Keiton scored fifty-three points, hitting eleven of fourteen three-pointers. Fans of high school basketball were in awe. They couldn't wait to see Pawnee's offense match up against the Saints' defense. It was being built up as the game of the year, and it was going to decide the 2A championship.

In the state final, it soon became clear that the Saints had the advantage. They moved the ball better than Pawnee and included everyone on the court. It was a true team effort. Blake and his teammates George Overbey, Tucker Phillips, and Wilson Holloway all scored in double digits. The Saints out-rebounded the Black Bears thirty-seven to fifteen. Keiton did everything in his power to keep the game close, scoring a game-high thirty-four points and adding two rebounds. He had a great game—but it wasn't enough to stop Blake and the Saints.

When the final whistle blew, it was a blowout. The Saints had won their fourth straight state title, by thirty-one points.

"Words can't describe how this feels," said Blake, who finished his high school career with a twenty-two-point, seven-rebound, six-assist night. "This is what we've been working for all along. A lot of people overlook the other players on this team, but we showed we've got five guys who can score."

Blake and the Saints had made history. Blake was named the Class 2A MVP, while teammates Holloway, Overbey, and Phillips were named to three of the five spots on the all-tourney team.

Blake won almost every award there was that year, including Little All-City and Oklahoman Super 5. He was also named to the McDonald's All-American team and, in late March, went to Louisville to play in the biggest game for high school basketball players. Blake had an off game, only scoring four points for the West team, but he did win the dunk contest with an array of dazzling feats of athleticism. The slam-dunk championship capped a historic high school career that could be considered one of the greatest of all time. It was amazing what Blake had accomplished in four years, and everyone hoped it was only a taste of what was to come.

Joe Murphy/Getty Images

BLAKE GOES UP FOR THE REBOUND AGAINST GANI LAWAL AND
NOLAN SMITH OF THE EAST TEAM DURING THE BOYS' MCDONALD'S
ALL-AMERICAN HIGH SCHOOL BASKETBALL GAME.

CHAPTER FIVE
2007–2008

FAMILY REUNION

For Blake, the sometimes tough transition from high school to college was made easier since he had often been to the campus in Norman, Oklahoma, to visit Taylor. Blake already knew many of his teammates from playing pickup games, and even knew his way around the campus a bit—and for what he didn't know, he had Taylor to show him the ropes. Taylor, already a junior, knew how long it would take to get to morning team meetings, when practices and workouts were, and the ins and outs of the training routine.

Blake had more structure than most incoming freshmen because of basketball. There were team meetings, practices, and weight training. To make sure he could play in his first season, the coaches checked in on Blake's classes to make sure he did well and continued to maintain his academic eligibility. The University of Oklahoma really needed Blake to be comfortable and play his best. Because while Blake and Oklahoma Christian were winning their fourth state championship in a row, Taylor and the Sooners were not faring quite as well.

The 2006–2007 season was Jeff Capel's first as Oklahoma's head coach. Coach Capel did his best, but the team had failed to make the postseason for the first time in over twenty-five years, breaking the longest streak in Division I basketball. The Sooners also missed March Madness for the first time in eleven years and for only the fifth time since 1983. It was a tough year for both the players and the fans.

Coach Capel knew that his team was better than they had seemed the previous season, and he and the players were set on making this season very different. After a few warm-up games during a preseason tour through Canada, the Sooners hosted the University of San Francisco in the first round of the 2K Classic college hoops tournament. The Sooners went into the kickoff tournament unranked in the nation and only the fifth-ranked team in the Big 12 Conference. The previous season had not inspired any faith in the Sooners team, but Blake would change all that. And he started with his first game.

Blake scored the first points early in that game with a layup, and just moments later, Taylor scored

Oklahoma's next two points. Together, the Griffin brothers scored the first eight points of the 2007–2008 season, setting the tone for the rest of their year. Blake ended the game with a team high of eighteen points and thirteen rebounds in the first start of his college career, and Taylor dropped thirteen points and six rebounds, the second highest totals in both categories for the Sooners. It was Blake's first double-double in his crimson-and-cream uniform, and it would not be his last.

The Griffins grabbed nineteen of the team's thirty-five rebounds and thirty-one of its seventy-one points. It was a statement game for the brothers—and it announced to the college basketball ranks that the freshman from Oklahoma City was the real deal. Still, Blake knew that there was always room to get even better.

"I definitely need to play harder every possession, I have to keep my intensity up every play, and I have to be able to do that for a full forty minutes," Blake answered after being asked where he needed to improve. "I know that to be the player I want to be, I have to improve all facets of my game."

The brothers turned in another impressive outing in their next game, helping Oklahoma beat Denver by thirty points. Blake scored a game high of fifteen points, and Taylor added twelve. Despite scoring more points than anyone else in the game, and managing to throw down multiple monster dunks in only his second college game, Blake still felt he could have contributed more.

Coach Capel knew he needed to be a little tough on Blake to push him past his limits and to make him a better player. "Blake knows that I'm a lot harder on him than anyone," said Coach Capel. "I have very high expectations for Blake because I know what he can become, and I know what we need him to become for our team to get to the level where we want to be. Blake also has high expectations for himself. He's such a talented and good kid, but sometimes we forget because he's six-foot-ten, two hundred fifty-five pounds, and has seven percent body fat, that's he's eighteen years old and he's just playing his second game. I thought both of these games were great learning experiences for him and I know that he'll use it to get better."

Blake was indeed talented, but all across the country, extremely talented future NBA players and stars were starting out as freshmen, and Blake would have to face a series of them throughout the year. The season would be a trial for the super-talented freshman.

In the Sooners' next game, against Alcorn State, Blake scored sixteen points and grabbed eleven rebounds for his second double-double, and Oklahoma crushed Alcorn, 99–59. It was not a perfect game for Blake, but he was making progress.

Then the Sooners ran into a very talented Memphis Tigers team, led by future NBA superstar Derrick Rose, in the semifinals of the 2K Classic. This was the Sooners' first real test of the season, and Rose was the first of the very talented freshmen Blake would have to face.

The Tigers knew that Blake was Oklahoma's best player, so they focused their game plan on him. Memphis decided to do something they didn't normally do: they double-teamed Blake whenever they got the chance. Only three games into the season, the Sooners clearly relied on the six-foot-ten-inch freshman a lot—perhaps a little too much.

Memphis was able to hold Blake to only eight points and eight rebounds, while Derrick Rose led the Tigers with seventeen points. Rose was able to find lanes to the basket everywhere, and he slashed his way to the rim every chance he got. Memphis comfortably won the game by ten points. Still, Blake had gained the respect of everyone for holding his own against a team of that caliber, and for one massive dunk he made over Rose.

The Sooners breezed through the next two games. Blake recorded another double-double, his third in just six games. With every game, he became more of the focus of the Sooners' offense, and that put a bull's-eye squarely on his back. Every team was going to test him under the basket and play him physically to see if they could get in his head, break his rhythm, and disrupt his game. Blake had worn that same bull's-eye during his high school career when every opposing coach sent players to foul him as a way of trying to stop the power forward. It turned out that college wasn't that different.

In late November, the Sooners traveled to the West Coast for a Thursday matchup against the twenty-second-ranked University of Southern California. Oklahoma couldn't find an offensive rhythm against the high-powered Trojans' attack. With Blake off his game that night as well, the Sooners escaped a terrible first half and were down by only eleven going into the locker room. The Sooners played better in the second half, with both teams scoring thirty-seven points, but the eleven-point halftime deficit was too much for the Sooners to overcome. Blake had been very quiet offensively. He had a game-high nine rebounds, but could muster only four points on two shots out of four attempts, with zero trips to the free-throw line. This was not what Coach Capel was expecting from his freshman power forward. The Sooners were now 5–2, with losses in both of their matchups against ranked teams. While they had played well, Coach Capel knew they had missed opportunities to establish themselves that season.

Oklahoma would win three of their next four games, with big wins over Texas Christian University, Tulsa, and Arkansas. But Blake's hot start to the season had cooled considerably. He averaged fourteen points and only five and a half rebounds over those four games— not nearly enough for a player of his quality. Because of this, Blake failed to make the starting lineup for the Arkansas game. Coming off the bench had never suited Blake, and he made his intentions for the rest of the season known when he returned to the starting lineup to face eighteenth-ranked Gonzaga, the teams' first meeting in the All-College Classic.

Blake had fourteen rebounds, which helped the Sooners to a ridiculous plus-ten differential on the night, to go along with his two assists and two blocks. It was a balanced, tough, and consistent performance, and a great way to bounce back after being pulled from the starting lineup. OU would end up wearing out Gonzaga, and the Sooners won 72–68. It was a solid win against a strong program.

The Gonzaga game was a great win, and the next game against West Virginia was twice as good. It was also a better performance from Blake. He put together his first back-to-back double-double since the start of the season, and the frontcourt pairing of the talented six-foot-eleven-inch center Longar Longar and Blake began to play up to its potential.

In many ways, it was the play of the Sooners guards that made it possible for Blake and Longar to play the way they did. Austin Johnson and David Godbold created havoc for the West Virginia Mountaineers, who were ranked twenty-third in the nation. Blake got off to a good start that game. In the first half, he scored ten of the team's twenty-four points and was a handful under the basket, but it was Austin's and David's outside shooting and penetrating drives to the basket that kept the Mountaineers from crashing inside and double-teaming the Oklahoma frontcourt. Blake was pulling down second chances for the Sooners all game—he was getting sent to the free throw line as West Virginia fouled him underneath the basket in an attempt to stop him. Despite the Sooners' strong play, West Virginia and Joe Alexander's eleven first-half points had the Sooners down by three at halftime.

In the second half, Longar joined Blake in the attack and scored fourteen points. With just over six minutes to play, Alex Ruoff extended West Virginia's lead to 58–50 before OU went on a 7–0 run that was capped by one of Blake Griffin's nationally televised monster slams. The Mountaineers took a quick timeout to regroup, but it was clear the momentum had shifted. There was just over a minute left to play in the game when the Sooners took their first lead of the game after two free throws from Longar and a great back-to-the-basket move by Blake. With West Virginia down by two and just seconds on the clock, their star player, Joe Alexander, missed an easy shot to tie the game, but his teammate Alex Ruoff got a wild put-back to fall with just four seconds left. It had been a physical game, a real fight, but neither team had figured out a way to keep the lead. The Sooners and Mountaineers headed into overtime tied with a score of 66–66.

When the whistle blew, West Virginia scored first

and got out to a five-point lead, forcing Oklahoma to play the entire overtime from behind. Down 73–70 with only twenty-four ticks left, the Sooners seemed to be letting the game slip away—but Oklahoma's shooting guard drained three to send the game into double overtime.

However, the Sooners let WVU open the second overtime period with the same quick burst of scoring, and again they had to play catch-up. But the game changed when two Mountaineers fouled out, and then Blake fouled out with less than four minutes left in the final overtime. The whole tone of the game shifted. After that, Longar took full advantage of the Mountaineers' lack of size by scoring eight of the Sooners' final fifteen points. Oklahoma outlasted WVU to win 88–82 for their first road victory against a ranked opponent since early 2001.

After the game, Coach Capel was very excited about the win. He was so proud of his team. They had shown the nation what they were capable of when they played as a unit on both sides of the court. The victory brought the national spotlight back to Norman, Oklahoma. Talk of a Sooners appearance in the Top 25 began to swell in the ranks of the crimson-and-cream team.

For the first time in a long time, the Sooners fans had hope. They believed that this team might be more than just competitive and that Blake and his teammates might actually be good enough to make it to the NCAA Tournament. Maybe Blake Griffin was the type of player they had been waiting for those last few years. Judging by his performance against West Virginia when he scored a season high of eighteen points, added sixteen rebounds, notched his fifth double-double, and won his first Big 12 Player of the Week award—Blake was exactly as good as everyone thought he would be.

The Sooners won the next two games to push their record to 12–3 before opening Big 12 conference play against Kansas State. It was a tight game, and ultimately, the Kansas State Wildcats outplayed the Sooners to an 84–82 defeat. It was a tough loss for the Sooners—and on top of that, it snapped a five-game winning streak.

That game was hard fought, though, in part because of the Sooners freshman power forward, whose game was growing every time he played. Blake set a new personal high for points that game, and with his fourteen rebounds, the game marked his sixth double-double of the season. Coach Capel made sure everyone knew it, too, saying, "Blake is very good.... He did more than hold his own. He is as good as anyone in college basketball."

On January 14, 2008, the Sooners traveled to Lawrence, Kansas, to take on a third-ranked University of Kansas team that boasted five future NBA players, including Mario Chalmers. This was a stacked team, from the bench to the starters. They were big and fast—and they could shoot. The Jayhawks were so talented that it was hard to find a way to plan a game against them. It was the perfect opportunity for Blake to show the world what he could do against an elite program on the road.

As expected, the Jayhawks started the game fast and were very physical. Kansas scored the first nine points of the game, the first two coming from an impressive dunk. With five minutes gone, Blake went up for a rebound and landed on his left leg awkwardly. He fell to the ground and immediately clutched his knee.

He was taken directly to the locker room for further evaluation, and Taylor was subbed in from the bench. Without Blake, the scoring inside fell to Longar, and he responded with twenty-one points and five rebounds. Taylor, on the other hand, was rusty. He ended the game with eight boards and eight points, but he missed all four of his three-point attempts and shot only 18 percent in a season high of thirty-four minutes of action. Over the last six games, Blake had established himself as one of the team's leaders on and off the court. It was a huge blow for Oklahoma to lose their star player so early to an injury that could cost Blake his season. Between the Kansas State loss and Blake's injury, the Sooners were too deflated to get up for a game against a team of Kansas's quality.

The Sooners shot a season low 32.8 percent that night, and were out-rebounded by Kansas 40–31. They lost the game by thirty points. The toughest part was not knowing how bad Blake's injury was or whether he was going to be able to play again that season. Blake went in for an MRI the day after the game, and the doctors confirmed that it was a medial collateral ligament sprain. This injury didn't normally need surgery, but it could sideline Blake for a minimum of four weeks, maybe even longer.

"We're very glad it's not season ending or career threatening," said Capel. "But it's a huge blow to our team. Blake is our leading scorer and rebounder, and has been playing his best basketball. He was really starting to become the dominant player that we knew he could be." Coach Capel now had a six-foot-ten-inch-size hole in his frontcourt, and someone needed to step up to fill it while Blake was out. The best candidate for that role was, of course, Taylor.

Taylor showed he was up for the challenge in the very next game, where over the last eight minutes, he scored eleven of the Sooners' last twenty-two points and pulled in four of his twelve rebounds, helping Oklahoma beat Texas Tech, 63–61.

"I am really proud of the character that we showed and the manner in which we won after being down by seven. I'm really proud of Taylor Griffin. He stepped up and played well, and he did it with character," said Coach Capel.

Blake wanted to play. He was sure his knee was healed enough, so before the next game, every chance he got, he told Coach Capel that he was ready and had only needed one game to rest the knee, even though his doctors had said he'd need to sit out four games. Coach had seen Blake struggling in practice, so he was not fully convinced, even after the team doctors cleared Blake to play the morning of the game. In the end, Coach Capel decided to give Blake a few minutes on the court. He wouldn't start, but he would play.

The Baylor Bears had broken into the Top 25 ranking for the first time in thirty-nine years and were playing their best basketball, having just won a five-overtime thriller against Texas. Further, the Bears were looking for some payback after going winless in their last twenty-six matchups against Oklahoma. For their part, the Sooners, who had not lost to Baylor since 1977, felt pressure to keep up their winning streak.

Taylor started. He put in a great shift, but having Blake back really made all the difference. It gave the team an emotional boost. Blake ended up playing only twenty-two minutes, but he made every minute count. He was by far the best player on the floor that night, and even though he only made one of his four free throw attempts and missed a number of other shots, he scored seventeen points and added fifteen rebounds. Baylor hadn't expected him to play, and they didn't have a game plan for Blake's size under the basket. Oklahoma beat Baylor, 77–71.

Blake's performance didn't go unnoticed. For his efforts, he was named the Big 12 Player of the Week again, as well as the league's Rookie of the Week. Blake was averaging a double-double in conference play despite barely recording a point during the Kansas game. Blake would need to keep playing at his best, because the Sooners' biggest rivals were coming to town.

The Bedlam Series pitted the Oklahoma State Cowboys against the University of Oklahoma Sooners. In basketball, the Sooners had won four of the last six games and were 122–88 all time against the Cowboys.

It was clear that both of the Griffin brothers understood what was at stake. They both went into the game with the intention of fighting for every basket, setting every screen as hard as they could, and diving for every loose ball. With his injury lingering, Blake again started the game on the bench, leaving Taylor in for the tip. Once Blake was on the court, the Cowboys double-teamed him, leaving Taylor to have one of the best games of his college career. He had ten points by halftime, on his way to a career high of twenty points—but he had to scrap for every one.

Blake got only twenty-seven minutes that game, so he had to work to notch fifteen points. His biggest contribution was one of the most athletic plays of the game. David Godbold clanged a long three with just under a minute to play, and the score tied at 57–57. Blake jumped, twisted in the air, grabbed the ball from behind his head, and willed it into the basket all in one motion—while being fouled. Blake stepped to the line and drained one of his nine free throws in fifteen attempts to complete the three-point play, giving the Sooners a lead that they would not relinquish. Both teams traded late free throws until time ran out, and the Sooners beat the Cowboys 64–61.

It was a great game. The team celebrated for one night, but then it was back to work. The toughest portion of their season was still to come. With conference play heating up and matchups against Top 25 teams, the Sooners would have to play even better and tougher.

The team's momentum dried up quickly after the Oklahoma State game. They lost their next game to twenty-third-ranked Texas A&M, 60–52. Worse than the actual loss was the loss of the team's center. Three minutes into the game, the Sooners' second-leading scorer and rebounder, senior Longar Longar, landed awkwardly on his already injured right leg, which broke. Longar tried to play the rest of the Texas A&M game, but it was too painful.

Without Longar, Oklahoma lost their next two games, and the team felt completely deflated when they traveled to Colorado to play a struggling team that the Sooners should have easily beaten. Colorado tried to double-team Blake, but he broke through the defenders relentlessly to the tune of a game-high twenty-five points, five rebounds, and five assists. The problem, however, was that no one else on the Sooners was able to score more than nine points. They didn't lose because they were beaten—they beat themselves by not playing well. It was a low point of the Sooners' season.

Oklahoma followed those three losses with three much-needed wins. One of the biggest wins that season was the return of Longar from his leg injury—and he came back just in time for the Sooners' rematch against Baylor in Norman. They beat Baylor, 92–91, in overtime.

Those three wins were incredibly important, because after that, the Sooners had to face arguably the hardest stretch of their season. First up was Texas—the best team in the Big 12—at home, and then they'd travel to Nebraska to take on the Cornhuskers, and end up at home to play Texas A&M again.

University of Texas at Austin was after Oklahoma that season. The Longhorns had realized what most teams in the Big 12 had figured out: they could try to contain Blake Griffin, but the best they'd really be able to do was limit his touches. Blake put up a respectable sixteen points and sixteen rebounds, but the rest of the team was cold. The Sooners shot only 26.4 percent on the night and were out-rebounded 43–38. It was one of the most disappointing games for the Sooners, who scored a season-low forty-five points, and lost 62–45.

Four days later, the Sooners matched their season low in Nebraska. Again Blake played well, with seventeen points, on seven-for-eight shooting, and eight rebounds, but the rest of the team remained flat. The Cornhuskers shot 50 percent from the field and the Sooners shot 37 percent.

All of the frustration with their performances over those two games came pouring out onto an unsuspecting Texas A&M team. Oklahoma's defense kept the Aggies from scoring for more than sixteen minutes in the game, holding them to a low of thirty-seven points on the night. The 64–37 win for the Sooners was just what they needed to set the season right—and it came from a balanced attack. It wasn't just up to Blake. Three Sooners scored in the double digits: Longar scored fourteen points and had eight rebounds; Blake had thirteen points and added another eight rebounds; and Austin Johnson dropped thirteen points of his own. It was a true team win.

But it wasn't all good news: Blake had injured his

right knee during the game, when he was elbowed by one of the A&M players, lost his balance, and fell. The next day, Blake had a scan on his right knee. His left knee had already kept him out of two games, and he didn't want to miss any more. He was hoping to be able to just rest it, but the scans showed some structural damage—not enough to end Blake's season, but enough to keep him out of the second Bedlam Battle. After having surgery, Blake again tried to make a speedy recovery so that he could play, but in the end, he wasn't able to.

Blake wrote on a blog how hard he had tried to make the Bedlam game, even though it was just three days after his knee surgery. In the end, he watched on TV as his teammates won by twelve points.

The time off helped him make a complete recovery. Blake was back by the last game of the regular season, against Missouri, just a week later, and he came off the bench to contribute fourteen points and eight rebounds to the win. He struggled against Colorado in the quarterfinals of the Big 12 Tournament and was limited to fifteen minutes and four points, though he grabbed nine rebounds, which is a testament to his immense skill.

Blake was well enough to log some serious minutes

by the conference semis against Texas. He found a way to bring his A-game against his toughest opponents. The Longhorns tried to stop Blake as usual, and they made sure to shut down the rest of the team. But Texas was too good, and in the end, they bounced the Sooners from the Big 12 Tournament. Still, Blake and the Sooners finished the season with a 22–11 record that was good enough for an at-large berth to the NCAA Tournament. The Sooners were placed in the East Regional bracket as a sixth seed behind the University of North Carolina, Tennessee, University of Louisville, Washington State, and Notre Dame. Blake would be a part of the famous March Madness!

The first round of the tournament was in Birmingham, Alabama, and Oklahoma handled the eleventh-seed St. Joseph's squad, 72–64. In the next game, the Sooners faced the third-seed Louisville Cardinals. Coach Rick Pitino's game plan focused on Blake, and the Cardinals double-teamed Blake every time he touched the ball. They were going to pester Blake and keep him from getting into a rhythm—and it worked.

By the half, the Cardinals had built a twenty-two-point lead. At the final whistle, they had tallied an easy win of 78–48. It was a heartbreaking way to end the season, especially for the seniors on the team, who might never play on the national stage again. For Blake, it was motivation.

At the end of the season, Blake was named to the First-Team All-Big 12 squad for one of the best freshman seasons anyone in a Sooners uniform had ever played. He averaged 14.7 points and 9.1 rebounds, which ranked ninth and fourth, respectively, in the Big 12. His 56.8 field goal percentage was the third best from the floor in the league. He had racked ten double-doubles, while recording two Big 12 Player of the Week awards and one Rookie of the Week award. He had put together arguably the best freshman season since Oklahoma legend Wayman Tisdale's freshman year in 1982–1983.

For Blake, though, the end of the college basketball season meant the beginning of a big decision. His play had attracted the attention of the NBA, and there were rumors he could be a lottery pick, but he wasn't sure he was ready to leave college yet. He had only a few weeks to decide whether he should go to the NBA, or stay in college and shoot for a national championship.

CHAPTER SIX
2008–2009

THE GRIFFIN BROTHERS' LAST STAND

Soon after Blake's first season ended, Coach Capel was given a two-year contract extension because of the success he had brought to the program. To sustain the progress of the last season and, hopefully, build on it, Coach Capel needed to keep Blake, who was getting lots of attention from the NBA—but he also needed to do right by his star player.

After an outstanding freshman year, people thought that Blake would be between the third and tenth pick if he declared for the draft, which could mean a $10 million paycheck for him and his family. That was a lot of money to say no to, and it could all disappear if he decided to stay in school and was injured enough to not be able to play professionally. At the same time, Blake played because he loved the game—he loved playing with his brother, and he loved playing for Oklahoma and Coach Capel. He loved playing in front of his mother, his father, and his friends.

There was risk with either choice, making it a tough decision. Blake said as much during his press conference on April 9, 2008, to announce his decision: "It was tough at first, because going to the NBA has been my dream for as long as I can remember," Blake admitted. "And that opportunity presented itself, but once I sat down and went over the pros and cons, the decision was a little bit easier than I thought."

In the end, his family helped him make his final decision. Taylor and Blake spoke at length about what he should do and whether they had accomplished all their goals. And they decided they hadn't.

"My brother gave me some advice in terms of the pros and cons of leaving—what would be good, what would be bad," Blake told the press. "I respect him and look up to him, and he had an effect on me in terms of my decision. . . . Our team has a chance to be really good next year. We want to be one of the top teams in the country and make a statement with what we're trying to do as a program. I also want to get a lot better this summer so that I can be in a better [draft] position than I am now."

Many of that year's super-talented freshmen declared for the draft: Memphis's Derrick Rose, Kansas State's Michael Beasley, USC's O.J. Mayo, UCLA's

Kevin Love, and Indiana University's Eric Gordon were all drafted in the first seven picks. Blake had decided to buck the trend. It was a decision that would pay off for the young man from Oklahoma City.

With Blake deciding to stay another year, the Sooners' prospects shot through the roof. The team was widely considered to be the favorite to win the Big 12 that season. The Sooners were ranked in Top 25 preseason polls, with the AP ranking them as high as twelfth, which was ahead of Texas and Kansas, two of last season's best Big 12 teams. The next season was shaping up to be something special.

The 2008–2009 season featured three of the most talented players to ever play college ball, whose play captured the attention of the whole country. Tyler Hansbrough, future NBA MVP Stephen "Steph" Curry, and Blake Griffin made that season more exciting with every game they played, breaking multiple college basketball records along the way. All three players were nominated to the preseason AP All-American list and were expected to vie for the national Player of the Year award.

Blake had used the loss to Louisville during the NCAA Tournament to push him over the summer. He had worked out harder, played more games, and focused on his shooting and post moves. Because of his hard work, he had put on almost ten pounds of muscle. He had also added a few new moves. He had been working on his jumper that summer, and Blake began the season with a new confidence in his midrange shot and his deep ball. Coach Capel also encouraged his star forward to start shooting from the outside. He wanted Blake to get comfortable with his outside shooting in a real game situation. Now every team would have to plan for both Blake's inside and outside games.

The Sooners had a healthy and super-strong Blake to lead their team, and that season they added another weapon: Willie Warren, a five-star recruit from Texas who had had great success on the high school courts. Willie was now a second offensive option for which teams would have to game-plan. Tasked with replacing the points lost with the graduation of Longar Longar and David Godbold, Willie excelled as the outside shooter for the Sooners that season.

The beginning of every season's schedule is usually front loaded with easy nonconference games for many of the blue-chip programs. That year, Oklahoma started with American and then Mississippi

Valley State. A night later, the Sooners clashed with Davidson. Most seasons, the Wildcats would have been an easy win for the Sooners and a perfect warm-up game to start the season—but not that year. Not with Steph Curry on the Davidson squad.

Steph was most of the Davidson offense, as he had put up twenty-nine and thirty-three points in the previous two games. The Sooners would need both Blake and Willie that night and some spectacular playing by Taylor to beat Steph Curry. Lucky for Oklahoma, Steph didn't play as well as he had before. He shot only 41 percent and missed nine of fifteen three-pointers—but he still dropped forty-four points on Oklahoma that night. Steph had single-handedly kept Davidson in the game. Even on an off night, he was capable of turning in a Player of the Year performance.

For all the points that Steph scored, Blake and Oklahoma put in a complete team performance. The first half ended with Oklahoma up 38–34. Blake grabbed eleven rebounds in the second half, and after every rebound, the Wildcats purposely fouled him. His free throw percentage had gotten better since high school, but it was still one of the weakest parts of Blake's game—a fact that Davidson was counting on.

Unfortunately for the Davidson team, Blake hit free throw after free throw that night, making eleven out of twelve, all in the second half. Steph made fourteen out of fourteen free throws that night, but Blake's new skill took Davidson by surprise.

With thirteen minutes left in the game, Blake had dunked the Sooners to a twenty-one-point lead, but Steph snapped out of his early second-half slump and scored nine points in a 14–0 run by the Wildcats, beginning their comeback. Davidson players started running screen after screen, getting Steph the ball in the corners and at the top of the key. When Steph didn't have a shot, his vision on the floor allowed him to set up teammates for an easy two.

All Oklahoma could do was try to absorb the attack and put up as many points as possible, weathering the flurry of shots by Steph, who scored twenty-three points.

Once the momentum shifted, it seemed like the Sooners couldn't catch a break. Davidson pressed on defense and scrambled for every ball. Despite the onslaught, the Sooners were still up by fourteen points with over five minutes to play in the game when the Wildcats started showing signs of wearing down. Many of them were either in foul trouble or had already fouled out. There weren't many subs left to play.

Blake uncharacteristically missed a defensive rebound, and then Sooners guard Austin Johnson turned the ball over trying to force it to the wing. Steph hit a deep three with Blake and a teammate in his face. On the next possession, Oklahoma bricked, then Davidson bricked—and when Blake grabbed the rebound, he was immediately tied up by a Davidson player. With a jump ball, the possession arrow pointed to Davidson. The Wildcats would get another chance, and Steph back-cut the Sooners for two.

Blake created some Sooners luck of his own with a sweet cross-court pass to Austin for an uncontested layup. After the play, Blake started flapping his arms with his palms facing the sky, wildly trying to get the fans back into the game, but Davidson hit another three to quiet the crowd again. Taylor hit two free throws just before Steph drilled a three-pointer from the corner with both Blake and Austin in his face. That shot cut the lead to three with just fifty-three seconds on the clock, and then a free throw gave the Sooners a four-point lead.

Davidson pushed the ball downcourt, trying to make a four-point play to tie the game with seventeen seconds on the clock. Steph forced a pass that was deflected, and Taylor jumped toward the line, palming the ball to his brother. Blake took the ball, drove the length of the court, and slammed the ball home to put the exclamation point on the game. The basket was ruled to have happened just after the buzzer, but it didn't matter. Blake was making a statement with that play. The crowd roared. Blake clenched his fists and let out a scream that shook the arena's rafters.

It wasn't a perfect game for either team. It was a gutsy, gritty game. Blake and the Sooners had held off a talented team, and they had done it with a wide range of offense and some timely, physical defense. Blake finished the game with twenty-five points and a career-high twenty-one rebounds, but his 63.6 shooting percentage and his free throw shooting were what he was most proud of that night. Willie scored twenty points, and Taylor added sixteen.

It was clear to everyone who watched that game—including the other team—that the Sooners were built to make a deep run in March, especially if Blake and Taylor continued to play together the way they had that night. That season was likely the Griffin brothers' last stand, and they were going to enjoy every minute.

The rest of that early season nonconference schedule wasn't much easier than the Davidson game. Blake continued to improve over the season, and the Sooners played well—well enough to get a trip to the semifinal game of the National Invitation Tournament (NIT) Season Tip-Off. It was the first time the Sooners had advanced to New York for the final rounds of the tournament.

Blake put on another show in New York against the University of Alabama at Birmingham with thirty-two points and fifteen rebounds, before meeting the tenth-ranked Purdue Boilermakers in the NIT Finals. A win would certainly push the Sooners into the top ten. The question on everyone's mind was, can Purdue stop Blake Griffin? Blake was averaging 27.2 points per game, and he led the country with his 18.8 rebounds per game. He was a one-man wrecking ball.

Nick Laham/Getty Images

TAYLOR AND BLAKE WALK DOWNCOURT DURING A GAME AGAINST THE PURDUE BOILERMAKERS.

"Our team has to know that Blake is going to get double-teamed, he's going to get triple-teamed, they're going to get physical with him. You can't force it. Other guys have to step up," said Coach Capel.

Purdue started the game exactly as expected. They were physical with Blake, and they planned to press the Sooners higher up the court and drop a man inside to cover Blake if the guards got free. The plan worked for a while. They were able to limit

Blake's touches and, ultimately, his influence on offense for long stretches. This also left Willie Warren open on the outside.

Each team played to its strengths and fought as hard as it could for some early-season hardware. The Sooners had the inside game, and the Boilermakers were sharpshooters. Blake was the force on the inside for Oklahoma. His size and strength were a major part of his game. Opposing teams might try to stop him early, but he would always wear them down, and by the end of the game, he would start a late offensive surge and power the Sooners to victory. That game against Purdue was no different. Blake started slowly, as he often did, and the lead changed hands ten times, with Purdue getting ahead by as much as nine at one point. It wasn't until late in the second half that Oklahoma made their surge.

With the better part of four minutes left to play, the Sooners noticed Purdue's passes weren't as crisp and their runs weren't as quick. The Boilermakers were getting sluggish. Oklahoma knew they had to make their move.

Taylor started the run with two great plays on both ends of the court. With the Boilermakers using their big man to set a high pick at the top of the key, pulling Blake out of the paint where he had been so successful, the job of crashing the lane fell to Taylor late in the game. Purdue tried to set the pick, but Blake saw it coming and was able to drop and clog the lane, while Taylor left the man he was marking to come in on the weak side for a nasty block. Taylor then ran the length of the court to tip in a Willie Warren miss.

Those two plays brought the game to within three points, effectively changing the momentum. Blake chipped in with a highlight moment of his own when Keaton Grant air-balled a shot for Purdue: Blake snatched the rebound and one-handed the ball the length of the court, hitting a streaking Austin in stride for an easy two points. It looked like a pass from quarterback to wide receiver rather than something you would expect to see during a basketball game. Blake's awareness of the game had matured steadily through his time at Oklahoma, but it was clear that year that he had really taken another step, with this play as a great example of his rising basketball IQ. That bucket tied the game at 69 and capped a 7–0 run for the Sooners.

The play intensified as both teams fought to come

out on top, and Oklahoma players were sent to the line again and again in the final seconds. The last six points for Oklahoma came from the line as the Sooners outlasted Purdue to win 87–82 and give the school its first NIT Season Tip-Off title.

Blake, Taylor, and Willie Warren all had good games, but it was a high-energy, team-effort win for the Sooners. Willie had a game high of twenty-two points, Taylor added nineteen points, and Blake tallied a game high of twenty-one rebounds, though he fell short of his season scoring average with only eighteen points that night. It was his sixth double-double of the season.

"It was a tough game for Blake," Coach Jeff Capel said. "And I hate to say that when he had eighteen and twenty-one, but they did a really good job of doubling him and being physical with him. He did a good job of being patient and trusting his teammates."

After that game, Blake was named the Big 12 Player of the Week for the third straight week and the tournament MVP, while Willie was awarded Rookie of the Week for the second week in a row. In total, five Sooners had scored double-digit points that game, proving they could grind out a tough win against a very talented team. They also proved that they were a much more balanced team than many had expected. They had a bench capable of contributing. The Sooners were a real threat and just might be good enough to challenge for a title come March.

The Sooners jumped in the polls from eleventh to sixth in the nation. It was the school's highest ranking since 2005. However, there was also an unwritten rule in college basketball: the higher your ranking, the more of a target you have on your back. The Sooners would have to prove themselves worthy of such a ranking every time they played.

The Sooners went on to win the next six games before losing their first game, to Arkansas. They then won the next thirteen games, including eleven straight conference games.

The Sooners team was ranked second in the nation when Blake had the best game of his career. He scored a career high of forty points and grabbed twenty-three rebounds. He shot 72.7 percent that night. He dunked over everyone—more than once. And if he couldn't dunk, he just posted up. Texas Tech coach Pat Knight likened him to a robot after the game. It was Blake's twenty-second double-double, breaking the school's record for double-doubles in a season.

Unfortunately, in the next game, Blake was pulled after he collided with a Texas Longhorns player under the basket and took a knock to the head. Due to concussion protocols, he left in the first quarter and never returned; then he was held out of the Kansas game that followed as a precautionary measure. Without Blake in those games, the Sooners' season took a downturn. They lost three of their last five games—to Texas, Kansas, and Missouri.

Oklahoma slid from second to fourth in the national rankings, ending the regular season with a 27–4 record overall and only three losses in conference play. Most important, the Sooners beat Oklahoma State, 82–78, in the last game of the season for their fifth consecutive win over their in-state rivals. Kansas won the Big 12 regular season, the Sooners were second, and Missouri finished with the third-best conference record that season. All three would be going to the NCAA Tournament.

Blake had played well all season. He followed every difficult game with a fantastic one, and he led the Big 12 Conference in points, shooting percentage, and rebounds. He averaged 22.1 points and

14.2 rebounds per game, shooting 63.4 percent. His 425 rebounds set a Big 12 regular-season record, and his twenty-five double-doubles were the most in school history. He was a unanimous Big 12 First Team selection and was ultimately named Big 12 Player of the Year. Then more Player of the Year awards started to trickle in. *Sporting News* named him its Player of the Year, and he was also named the Adolph Rupp Player of the Year.

But Blake's biggest challenge was yet to come. He wanted to take his team deep into the NCAA Tournament and challenge for a national title.

CHAPTER SEVEN 2009

MARCH MADNESS

It was rare for the two Oklahoma teams to meet in the postseason, and even rarer for them to play the game in Oklahoma City. But that season, the Big 12 Tournament was held in OKC, and the University of Oklahoma Sooners faced the Oklahoma State Cowboys, so the Ford Center was packed with fans wearing crimson and cream on one side, and black and orange on the other.

The atmosphere was electric. Before the game even started, the crowds were chanting and singing—and once the whistle blew, that intensity translated to the players.

The Cowboys' game plan was the same as every other team's: stop Blake with two or three players, and hope that the Sooners guards wouldn't hit their outside shots. "Blake Griffin, I just told my staff, may be the best player I've ever gone against as a player or a coach," said Cowboys coach Travis Ford before the game.

Both teams built leads that evaporated as the other team made improbable runs. The Sooners tied the score four times in the final six minutes, keeping the game tight, but guard Byron Eaton hit a free throw to put OSU up by one with twenty-nine seconds to go. On the last two plays, the referees made two controversial calls in favor of the Cowboys. Blake got a chance at one last shot as time ran out: it looked like he was fouled, and he expected to get a chance on the free throw line—but the Sooners didn't get that call, either. OSU beat the Sooners, 71–70, knocking them out of the conference tournament.

Everyone had underperformed for the Sooners. Blake got his double-double on seventeen points and nineteen rebounds, but he was well short of his average point total. The Sooners hit only 15.8 percent of their three-pointers and gave away nine more turnovers than the Cowboys.

The loss cost the Sooners the first seed spot in the NCAA Tournament, but the second seed in the South Regional bracket was not a bad place to be. The only problem was that OU was in the same bracket as North Carolina and Tyler Hansbrough, arguably the best team in the country and the defending Player of the Year.

Coach Capel had no desire to worry about UNC yet. It was time to regroup and focus on the start of March Madness. The Sooners' first-round game was against fifteenth-seed Morgan State in Kansas City. Oklahoma took an early 12–5 lead as Blake blazed a path inside with ten points. The Sooners slowly but surely opened the lead as the game went on, and Blake was an efficient machine despite the frequent physical play from Morgan State. In thirty-one minutes, Blake scored twenty-eight points and grabbed thirteen rebounds—another double-double. Taylor added eighteen points, and the Griffin brothers carried their team into the second round.

Just days before the Sooners' second game, against Michigan, Coach Capel was named a finalist for the Naismith Men's College Coach of the Year. It was a great honor to even be included as a finalist, and a testament to the great job he had done rebuilding the Oklahoma program. Soon afterward, Blake was, as everyone expected, also named a Naismith Trophy finalist for Men's College Player of the Year.

Michigan, only the tenth seed, had already upset

the seventh-seed Clemson Tigers in the first round, and the Wolverines intended to get past Oklahoma, too. Most opponents double-teamed Blake, and the Wolverines weren't taking any chances and glued two players to him wherever he went. There was only one problem with the Michigan game plan: two players weren't enough to stop Blake.

Every time he got the ball in the low post, he was mobbed—but that didn't make a difference. If they gave him an inch of the baseline, he spun below the trap and powered it home. When double-teamed on the high post, he set a pick on both players and let a guard streak to the basket for an easy two points. It must've been hard to score with two players draped all over him, but somehow Blake was able to create the smallest amount of space, separate himself from his defenders, and put the ball in the basket. While he actually missed six of the twenty shots he took and half of his ten free throw attempts, he also made quite a few impossible shots.

With the Sooners up by ten and just over nine minutes left in the game, Blake caught a pass midcourt, took three steps, and elevated so high that his elbow was above the rim. Wolverine Zack Novak tried to take the charge and almost had his feet set, but Blake twisted his body in the air, rattled the rafters with a nasty one-handed dunk, and drew the foul.

That dunk knocked the life out of any Michigan comeback, and the Sooners won the game by ten points. Blake put up thirty-three points and scratched out seventeen rebounds. The double-doubles just kept coming.

Blake was going to put up his numbers every game, but the team needed to perform if they were going to make it past their Sweet 16 matchup with Syracuse.

Jonny Flynn was having an outstanding season for the Orangemen. A former New York State Mr. Basketball out of Niagara Falls, Jonny Flynn was the Big East Tournament's MVP, despite Syracuse's loss to Louisville in the finals. Flynn was a scoring machine. He was averaging more than seventeen points, over six assists, and at least one amazingly play per game. For a six-foot guard, he could jump amazingly high. He was also fearless.

Blake continued a new trend he'd developed: he started the Syracuse game fast. He helped the Sooners build a quick eight-point lead on a sweet alley-oop from Austin Johnson. The third-seed

Orangemen would fight to within one point at the eight-minute mark, but the Sooners slowly pulled away through the rest of the half.

Blake had his terminator moment just before the half ended. Blake got the ball in transition on the right side of the midline. Syracuse only had time to drop two guards into the paint. Blake immediately recognized the mismatch and drove straight to the basket. Jonny Flynn stepped into Blake's path, crossed his arms at his waist, closed his eyes tight, and tried to get his feet set before the powerful forward hit him. Blake elevated like he was going to smash into Jonny, but he simply twisted and rolled the ball into the hoop. The impact lifted Jonny Flynn completely off his feet, and he landed hard on his back. The referee saw the slightest amount of movement and called Flynn for the foul. Blake got his "and-one" moment, and the Sooners went into the locker room with a thirteen-point lead.

The game didn't get better for Syracuse. Jonny Flynn wasn't the same after his encounter with Blake. He had a badly bruised back and fought through the pain to post a respectable twenty-two points and add six assists, but it wasn't enough to stop Blake and the Sooners. The lead quickly swelled to twenty points in the second half, and though the Orangemen pulled to within thirteen, by the end of the game, they lost to the Sooners, 84–71.

What really helped Blake's game that night was the fact that Sooners guard Tony Crocker was on fire from the outside, which forced Syracuse to keep a man on Tony. Without having to worry about always having that extra man on him, Blake was unstoppable on the inside. Blake led the game with thirty, but Tony was close behind with twenty-eight points.

The way Oklahoma was taking care of teams in the tournament, they looked capable of challenging the juggernaut North Carolina Tar Heels in the Elite 8 contest. Both teams came out tight to start the game. Balls were short, long, or off target completely. Players came up empty on buckets that had been automatic all season. It was a sloppy affair for the first few minutes, and it took two minutes for the Tar Heels to score their first field goal.

Then, things shifted. In the midst of nerves and broken plays, UNC built themselves a lead the hard way: the Sooners had committed five team fouls and were down 9–2 when, five minutes in, the Tar Heels drew two more quick fouls by pushing the ball in transition.

The Sooners were trying to slow the game down at the start and run set plays to break down the Tar Heel man-to-man defense. These plays were designed to force UNC to collapse on Blake Griffin with double- or triple-teams, freeing up the guards on the outside. This had been the Sooners' recipe for success all season, but the guards had to hit their shots to make it work, and that game, they went cold. Blake struggled to establish himself as a force inside for much of the start of the game, and instead of muscling out of the doubles and driving to the basket, he passed the ball, deferring to his teammates.

Tyler Hansbrough wasn't doing much better: he played only nine minutes in the half after picking up some quick fouls. UNC had dropped a number of hints that the expected battle between Tyler and Blake would not happen, and it was clear that the Tar Heels had the deeper bench. UNC coach Roy Williams's plan was to wear out the Oklahoma starters, throwing as many big bodies as possible at Blake. Tyler Zeller, Deon Thompson, and Ed Davis all spent time helping Hansbrough contain the Sooners star.

Over eleven minutes into the game, Blake finally tallied his first points. He kept trying to post up players down low, but with two or three players all over him, Blake was forced to put up bad shots or was stripped of the ball entirely. Blake scored eleven points in the first half, but five of them came from the foul line. Down 32–23 after twenty minutes, the Sooners needed Blake to get more looks, and to do that, Oklahoma had to hit their jumpers. Twenty-three points in the first half was a season low for the Sooners. Willie Warren was one for five during that span, and Austin Johnson didn't score, despite doing a great job locking down UNC's Ty Lawson. The Tar Heels just had too many strengths.

Every time the Sooners tried something new, like switching to zone from man-to-man, the Tar Heels found a way to break down the Oklahoma defense. The Tar Heels led by as many as fourteen points, and the Sooners never really challenged. Blake got his final double-double of the season with twenty-three points and sixteen rebounds, but the real story of the game was that Oklahoma had made only two out of nineteen shots from beyond the arc. It hadn't been that the shots weren't there, but that the Sooners had missed them. It was a devastating time for the guards to lose their confidence, and it turned the Sooners into a one-dimensional team. Oklahoma lost, 72–60.

North Carolina would go on to win against Villanova and then beat Michigan State in the national championship game. The Sooners had been unfortunate to run into the Tar Heels when they did. While it wasn't much consolation, the Sooners *had* managed to hold the powerhouse Tar Heels to their lowest point total of the tournament and their second lowest that season. The Sooners might have been the only ones capable of stopping that Tar Heels team—if their shots had fallen true.

After the season was over, Blake kept winning every award he was eligible for: he was named the Big 12 Male Sportsperson of the Year, as well as the AP Player of the Year. He was a unanimous AP All-American, and he won the Oscar Robertson Trophy, the Naismith Trophy, and the John R. Wooden Award. He had led the Sooners to a 30–6 record and to the Elite 8 bracket, while averaging 22.7 points, 14.4 rebounds, and 2.3 assists. Blake had had one of the best college seasons of all time, and he would be the consensus number one pick in the NBA draft if he chose to leave college. His stock would never be higher, but he hadn't brought Oklahoma the championship he had always dreamed of winning.

CHAPTER EIGHT
2009–2010

NBA: YEAR ONE

Blake thought about his future for a long time after his sophomore season ended. He talked to his mom and dad, Coach Capel, and his brother. Taylor was a senior and had used all four years of eligibility, meaning he had to either go pro or stop playing altogether. Even knowing Taylor wouldn't be on the team, Blake still had a tough time making his decision.

If Blake stayed, it would be to complete another academic year as well as to challenge for a title and bring home trophies to Oklahoma. On the other hand, perhaps with his brother leaving and his prospects as bright as they would ever be, it was time to move on.

He thought about it and thought about it, and in the end, he was too excited about the chance to play in the pros. He decided he would declare for the

NBA draft. At his press conference in early April, Blake talked about why he had made the choice.

"This past week, I have been going over in my mind what I should do," said Blake. "I sat down with Coach Capel and my family, and I think it is time for me to move on and take my game to the next level. It was tough. I love playing here—this is my home state. This is the school I wanted to come to.... It is tough to walk away from something like this, but at the same time, this is a big opportunity. I felt like I was ready for it this year, as opposed to last year."

It was a sad day for Coach Capel. He was clearly proud of his star player as he sat next to him at the press conference, but now he had some big shoes to fill. "[Blake] is probably one of the top two people I have ever been around and coached," Coach Capel said. "That is why I know he is going to be incredibly successful."

With the announcement out of the way, Blake's only focus was preparing for the NBA Draft Combine. The combine is where the top potential NBA draftees come together in one place to prove their skills and have their measurements officially taken. At the combine, Blake measured in at six feet ten inches and 248 pounds, with a six-foot-eleven-inch wingspan.

Also coming out that year was Arizona State's James Harden, Memphis's Tyreke Evans, and Spain's best prospect Ricky Rubio, as well as Jonny Flynn, Tyler Hansbrough, and Stephen Curry. It was a talent-heavy draft, and still Blake was the consensus best player in the draft year. Every mock draft had him as the first pick, and at the time, many pundits saw Blake as the only sure-fire prospect.

It is a great honor to be the first pick in the NBA draft. It means that player is the best one that year. However, it also means the player will be selected by one of the previous season's weakest teams, since the system allows the teams with the worst records to pick first. That year, the Los Angeles Clippers had earned the first pick with some really poor play. In fact, the Clippers had been bad for years.

Over the Clippers' forty-five seasons, the team had posted a losing record in thirty-four of them. This culture of losing dated back to when the franchise was known as the Buffalo Braves in the 1970s. Before the 1978–1979 season, the franchise had moved from New York State to San Diego and it changed names to the Clippers. The team moved again in 1984, this time to Los Angeles. Los Angeles already had a team, the Lakers, that had a championship pedigree and multiple titles, including a world championship just a few seasons before. The Lakers were one of the best-regarded and most successful franchises in professional basketball history. The Clippers were seen as second-rate, partly because they were moving from San Diego, the second largest city in Southern California, and partly because they always lost.

To top it all off, when Blake entered the draft, the Clippers were owned by Donald Sterling, who was frequently caught up in controversy. Sterling had bought the team in 1981, promising an immediate influx of money and spending that would change the fate of the Clippers franchise. Just a year later, he tried to move the team to Los Angeles. The Clippers were drowned in lawsuits, and the NBA started investigating how to force Sterling to sell the team. An NBA committee found that Sterling was late in paying players, had fallen behind paying his creditors and, at one point, had refused to pay a fan who had won $1,000 in a free-throw-shooting contest during a halftime promotional event. It didn't take long for Sterling to gain a reputation as a bad team owner.

In 1984, Sterling finally succeeded in relocating the team to Los Angeles, breaking the hearts of San Diego's Clippers fans. But the Clippers didn't get any better. It took eleven years for them to even post a winning record under Sterling's ownership. Still, despite the team's perpetual poor showings, 2009 was only the third time the franchise had gotten first pick in the NBA draft.

At the time of the 2009 draft, the Clippers hadn't finished higher than fourth in the Pacific Division and hadn't recorded over a .500 season for the past three years. During the 2008–2009 season, the Clippers managed only nineteen wins in eighty-two games and were tied with the Washington Wizards for the second-worst record, behind the Sacramento Kings. The Clippers were awarded the first draft pick through a weighted lottery that had been implemented in 1985 to give all non-playoff teams a shot at the number one pick.

With the number one pick, the Los Angeles Clippers selected Blake Griffin from the University of Oklahoma. It was the obvious choice. Both Griffin brothers had entered the draft, and the Phoenix

Suns selected Taylor with the forty-eighth pick in the second round.

For the Clippers fans, this was more than just a pick. Blake represented a new direction for a franchise that many fans believed was cursed. He represented hope for the Clippers team for the first time in years. A lot was riding on his shoulders.

The team had other talented players. The year before Blake was drafted, the Clippers drafted point guard Eric Gordon out of Indiana, and they had surrounded their two new stars with an experienced group of wily veterans. Centers Chris Kaman and Marcus Camby were charged with manning the rim alongside Blake, while guard Baron Davis hoped to regain his form in the backcourt.

The Clippers head coach and general manager, Mike Dunleavy, thought he had hit the jackpot with the Blake Griffin pick. Coach Dunleavy couldn't wait to see how Blake and Eric Gordon played together. Those two, along with center DeAndre Jordan, would make up the core of the Clippers 2009 Summer League team.

Blake started off his NBA career in typical Blake fashion: in his first Summer League game, he won the tip, backdoored the defense for an easy layup, hit a pretty twelve-foot fadeaway, and then swished a three-pointer for the Clippers' first seven points. It was just a taste of what Blake was capable of, but he had made it clear that his skills would translate to the NBA, and it left the Clippers fans cheering and hungry for more.

A shoulder injury caused Blake to miss part of the preseason, but it still looked like the power forward was ready to lead the Clippers to their first post-season appearance in years. Then Blake injured his knee in the final preseason game. He elevated for a dunk, lost his balance slightly in the air, and landed awkwardly on his left leg. It was only a stress fracture, but Blake would have to rest, and he would sit out the start of his first season. The fans weren't happy—maybe the Clippers really were cursed.

Injured or not, Blake was still a rookie, and as a way of welcoming players to the league, the veterans sometimes make rookies do silly things. As Blake was rehabilitating his knee that season, a photographer snapped a picture of him wearing an electric-blue-and-hot-pink Dora the Explorer backpack. A few days later, he was spotted still wearing the backpack. It was clear that this was part of Blake's initiation.

While everyone thought Blake would return after six weeks of resting his knee, doctors found that it wasn't healing correctly. In January 2010, he decided to have surgery, effectively ending his rookie season before it began. It was terrible news for Blake, the franchise, and the fans.

"It's a little disappointing, because he brings so much to the table," Coach Mike Dunleavy said. "As a group, we're coming together better all the time, and adding that talent to our lineup was something we were looking forward to. We've just got to move forward and do what we were planning on doing anyway—making the playoffs."

They didn't. Without Blake, the Clippers finished well out of playoff contention. The fans would have to keep waiting for their team to play postseason basketball. Midway through the season, Coach Dunleavy stepped down as head coach to concentrate on his general manager duties. Kim Hughes, Dunleavy's assistant, was named the interim coach for the rest of the season. A month later, Dunleavy was fired as the general manager. It was clear that change was in the air for the Clippers.

CHAPTER NINE
2010–2011

THE ROOKIE SEASON DO-OVER

Because his injury had occurred so early in the season, Blake retained his rookie status the following season. He was also reunited with a familiar face: the Clippers drafted a player from Oklahoma for a second straight year when they chose Willie Warren in the second round of the 2010 draft. They also drafted Al-Farouq Aminu, a small forward from Wake Forest. The team also added a few veteran pieces to fill out the roster.

That off-season, the Clippers front office hired Vinny Del Negro as the new head coach of the Los Angeles Clippers. Coach Del Negro had played pro ball overseas in Europe and with five different NBA teams, before retiring in 2001. He eventually became head coach of the Chicago Bulls and, until he was fired, took the Bulls to the postseason both years he was in charge.

Before the season started, everyone wanted to know

how Blake's surgically repaired knee was holding up. For the past year, fans and media alike had been reminiscing about Blake's final season in college when he was a double-double machine that scored points above the rim with thundering dunks and rebounded like a vacuum. Would he be the same player?

After a strong preseason, Blake's first game quieted everyone's doubts. During the season opener against the Portland Trail Blazers, Blake made the type of statement that put the whole league on notice—and he did it with his first basket. Just minutes into his first professional game of the regular season, Blake grabbed an alley-oop midair and smashed a year's worth of watching from the sidelines through the basket. He even landed awkwardly on his left leg, proving that he could still jump like a star and that his landing gear worked just fine.

That night, he unleashed an arsenal of offensive shots. His dunks practically shook the Staples Center, but it was Blake's ability to spin out of double-teams, catch the ball in traffic, and lay it in, plus his ability to launch sharp passes, that had the crowd in a frenzy by the end of the game. Blake got his first double-double that night with twenty points and fourteen rebounds, but the game ended with

Portland beating the Clippers, 98–88, and Blake wasn't happy with his performance or the result.

In the NBA, talent doesn't always translate into wins, and even with talented players, the Clippers only managed one win in their first fourteen games. Blake recorded a double-double in every one of the first twenty-three games. It was a great personal accomplishment, but all Blake was focused on was winning.

Something had changed in Blake's game during the time he spent rehabilitating his knee. Maybe a year of not playing ball had given the power forward too much time to think, or maybe it was because he was unleashing a year's worth of pent-up basketball after being away from the game for the first time in his life. Whatever the cause, Blake had a new fire in him. He'd always played hard, but there was something else to his game during his first professional year.

In late November, the New York Knicks were in Los Angeles to take on the Clippers. It was Blake's fourteenth NBA game, and he was still in the midst of his record-breaking twenty-three-game double-double streak. L.A. trailed by five at halftime and was kept in the game by Blake's stellar first-half play, but things started to slip away from the Clippers in the third quarter. Down by fourteen and looking to get something going for the Clippers, guard Randy Foye faked a shot, then hit Blake on the baseline. Blake turned, picked his head up, and drove to the basket. The Knicks seven-foot-one-inch rookie, Timofey Mozgov, quickly jumped into Blake's path and got his feet set. Blake had to make a decision within two bounces of the basketball: he could try a spin move, pass, or even pull up and shoot a short jumper. What Blake did shocked everyone. Blake nearly jumped over the New York center and threw the ball into the hoop! He tried to dunk, but he was too far away, so he threw a fastball through the basket. Mozgov had to protect himself, so he raised his arms, pushed Blake backwards, and fouled him.

"When he was driving to the hoop, I was ready to face him. I thought if something happens, I would foul him when the ball was low," said Mozgov after the incident. "But he's very quick! You can't imagine how quick he is. You say, take a charge or raise your arms? Before I had time to think, he was already up in the air. I understood that I only had time to give him a little push. I committed a foul, but because of that, he didn't jump over me."

Other people have dunked on seven-footers, but nobody before had done it with such raw force. The dunk was so powerful that Timofey's last name then became known as a proper noun *and* verb. When a player gets dunked on, people will say that the defending player was "Mozgov'd."

That dunk was simply the feather in Blake's cap. He scored twelve points in the first quarter and seventeen in the third on his way to forty-four points, fifteen rebounds, and seven assists. Blake exploded onto the scene to have the second best game of all time for a rookie, fifty years after Oscar Robertson put up forty-four, fifteen, and eleven. No one seemed to worry about Blake's knee anymore—the new question was, how good could Blake really become? Every game, he got better and more efficient.

By the All-Star Game, Blake was leading the league with 137 dunks and had the NBA buzzing about his determined play. His performance had earned him an All-Star reserve selection at the 2011 All-Star Game in Los Angeles.

Blake was an easy choice for inclusion in the Slam Dunk Contest that year. His first few dunks in the contest were good: one was a 360, and in the next, he lobbed the ball off the backboard before he crushed it through the net and hung by his elbow. Then there was his last dunk. Clippers guard Baron Davis climbed inside a new four-door Kia Optima automobile positioned just inside the paint and below the basket, opened the sunroof, and waited for Blake's signal. Then the Crenshaw Elite Choir came out onto the court and began to sing "I Believe I Can Fly." Blake ran straight at the car and soared into the air, caught a pass midflight that Baron Davis had thrown up through the sunroof, hung in the air for what seemed like an hour, and jammed the ball home. The maximum-capacity crowd at the Staples Center exploded with cheers, gasps, clapping, and laughter.

Pool/Getty Images Sport

BLAKE DUNKS OVER A CAR IN THE FINAL ROUND OF THE 2011 SLAM DUNK CONTEST.

When the fans voted on the winner of the 2011 Slam Dunk Contest, they selected Blake Griffin. It was a great honor, and it put Blake in some distinguished company, with past winners including Michael Jordan, Dominique Wilkins, Kobe Bryant, and Vince Carter.

On the winner's podium, Blake dedicated his Slam Dunk trophy to his best friend, Wilson Holloway. Blake and Wilson had met when they were fourteen years old, and they had become fast friends right away. As two goofballs who loved to laugh, Blake and Wilson played AAU basketball and won state championships together with Oklahoma Christian School. After graduating in 2007, Blake lit up the hard court for the Sooners, while Wilson mixed it up on the gridiron with Tulsa.

Then, in 2008, the unthinkable happened: Wilson was diagnosed with Hodgkin's lymphoma, a cancer that attacks the immune system. Wilson wasn't worried. He kept his cool. He knew what he had to do, and he was ready for the fight. His smile and laughter were his best weapons. Wilson went through multiple rounds of chemotherapy, and twice over the course of ten months, it seemed he had beaten the disease. He worked out with the Tulsa football team for as long as he could while he underwent treatment.

Wilson was fighting the second round of cancer

during the 2009 draft. His best friend was going to go number one overall, and Wilson wanted to be in New York City with Blake for the festivities. Wilson had just finished a round of chemo and was very weak, but he wouldn't take no for an answer. Even though he was ill, Wilson was there to watch his friend get picked by the Clippers.

During the start of the 2010 NBA season, Wilson's health began to worsen. Blake was in Minnesota playing the Timberwolves when he found out that Wilson had passed away. Blake cried in the locker room after the game. Three days later, with a heavy heart, Blake soared over the Kia to win the Slam Dunk Contest.

Blake continued to play his fantastic brand of basketball until the end of the season. Even so, the Clippers finished with a disappointing 32–50 record, and the team missed the playoffs again. Blake ended the year with thirty-five double-doubles, two triple-doubles, and a unanimous Rookie of the Year award.

Blake's play had given Clippers fans just enough hope to get excited about the next season. Maybe he was the player who would break the Clippers curse. For his part, Blake wasn't willing to continue to lose games. Something had to change. He decided to work harder and get even better.

CHAPTER TEN
2011–2012

THE LOCKOUT SEASON

In sports, the focus is often entirely on the athletes, and not the people behind the scenes who do the day-to-day jobs that make it all happen. But it takes quite a few people to make the show go on, and like all professional sports, basketball is also a business. Money pays the employees, keeps the stadium in working order, and drives many of the decisions for every sports franchise.

The NBA claimed that it lost over $300 million over the course of the 2010–2011 season. Players made a lot of money through their salaries, so the owners of the NBA wanted to pay the players less, while the players wanted to be paid more. Teams in smaller cities wanted more help from those in larger cities. Revenue sharing, hard versus soft salary caps, and many complicated issues were all in contention. The bottom line was that even after working on an agreement for over a year, the players and the NBA couldn't agree on how the league should handle its money.

In the past, when the two sides had disagreed, they had come to an understanding by negotiating a compromise on each and every issue. This compromise would be written down in the form of a contract known as a Collective Bargaining Agreement (CBA), which would last for a number of years. On July 1, 2011, after the end of the NBA season, the agreement expired. The players and owners needed to come to another compromise and draft a new CBA before basketball could be played again.

During that off-season, it was clear that the two parties were far from a compromise, and neither side wanted to give in. Frustrated by the players' unwillingness to negotiate, the owners of the NBA's thirty-two teams voted to institute a league-wide lockout. This meant that the owners would keep the players from engaging in any official team activities—including doing off-season workouts, using the team facilities, and even talking with coaches—until an agreement could be reached.

It had to be discouraging for Blake to be off the court after such a strong first season in the NBA, but he dealt with this situation the way he handled everything: with a smile and a great sense of humor. A few months into the lockout, Blake was finding other ways to occupy his time, the first being an opportunity to intern with actor Will Ferrell's comedy website, Funny or Die. At twenty-two years old, he was the same age as most of the other interns, and while he was there, he helped write, shoot, edit, and act in funny videos that featured athletes, including fellow NBA All-Star Kevin Love, Metta World Peace (formerly known as Ron Artest), and NFL running back Adrian Peterson.

As the summer of 2011 came to a close, the players and owners were not any closer to reaching a deal. It seemed that some of the season would be lost when talks continued to break down through September, and the risk of losing an entire year's salary was too much for many players. Some began to look to leagues in Europe and China for work, with many signing contracts that included an opt-out clause, which would allow them to return to the NBA should the league resume play. Players like Nicolas Batum, Ty Lawson, Serge Ibaka, Tony Parker, Danny Green, and even Kobe Bryant signed contracts or played overseas. But for most

NBA players, the lockout was a waiting game. It was up to the owners and player representatives to come to some sort of agreement. But they couldn't, so in October, the NBA commissioner decided to cancel the start of the regular season.

When a major sports franchise misses games, the league and the players aren't the only ones who are hurt by the lack of business. Stadiums and arenas employ hundreds of people, as do the shops and restaurants inside. Even the businesses in the surrounding neighborhoods suffer. Everyone is affected by a major league sports work stoppage. The NBA needed to figure this out soon to avoid missing an entire year. The league would also need to allow for some type of preseason to get the teams ready to start league play again.

It took all of November for the two sides to come to an agreement, and it wasn't until December 8 that the owners and players actually signed the new ten-year CBA. When it was all over, the 2011 NBA lockout had lasted a total of 161 days. The season's first games were scheduled for Christmas Day.

With the lockout over, teams started having training camps, and free agency was allowed to begin so players not under contract could move to new teams. The league agreed to a trade that would send Hornets point guard Chris Paul and a pair of second-round draft picks to the Clippers in exchange for a number of Clippers players. It was the biggest deal in Clippers franchise history.

Landing Chris Paul was a huge victory for the Clippers. He was a massive upgrade at point guard, one of the most sought-after skill positions on the court. Over the first six years of his career, Chris averaged 21.1 points per game, but it was his ability to unlock the opponent's defense that made him truly special. Chris had averaged ten assists a game while in New Orleans, where his no-look passes, behind-the-back moves, and alley-oops had wowed the fans and helped his teammates get easy and open shots at the basket. Chris Paul made everyone around him better.

And now Chris was going to play with a young power forward who could draw defenders to the low post and open Chris up to make even more plays. To prove his commitment to the Clippers, Chris immediately triggered his player option for the final year of his contract. He would be sticking around for at least two seasons.

Along with Blake and Chris, the Clippers also had DeAndre Jordan, Caron Butler, and veteran Chauncey Billups. This team was overflowing with talent—perhaps more talent than the Clippers ever had—but the question was whether that would translate into wins and a spot in the postseason.

The season started off sloppy, but well. Chris Paul's pinpoint passes had turned the Clippers into a high-flying circus of dunks and alley-oops. Blake had made a passing comment when Chris Paul was traded to the Clippers that it was "going to be Lob City." That nickname caught fire with the fans, and before long, everyone was calling the team Lob City. Fans chanted it. It even ended up on hats and shirts.

The pieces began to come together quickly for the Clippers after the rocky start. The new-look starting lineup would drive them to win six of seven, including an overtime victory against the Eastern Conference champions, the Miami Heat. That was the most balanced game the Clippers had played in a long time. Each starter contributed on offense and defense, and Chris Paul led the team with twenty-seven points and eleven assists, while Blake added twenty points and ten rebounds. DeAndre Jordan was the only starter who did not score double digits, but he had a monster game defensively: eight of his eleven rebounds came on defense, and he notched six blocks that hampered the Heat's rhythm and limited their scoring opportunities.

With Chris in town, the Clippers didn't rely on Blake to carry the team the way they had the season before. The balance on offense kept competing teams from zeroing in on Blake and double-teaming him, and on defense, Blake had some real help inside and a backcourt that could disrupt the play before the ball could be pushed inside.

The team was playing great for the first month of the season, but the Clippers lost Chauncey Billups to an injury in early February. The balance was immediately thrown off, and the Clippers went into a slump that threatened to ruin their season. Before Chauncey went down with the injury, they sat atop the Pacific Division and were second in the Western Conference, with a 15–7 record. Over the next twenty-five games, the Clippers lost fourteen times, and their record slipped to 26–21. Now they were second in the Pacific and tied for fifth in the West.

Finally, the Clippers went on a great run, winning fourteen of nineteen, starting with a six-game winning streak. They finished the season 40–26, a game and a half behind the Lakers for first place in the division. While not finishing better than the Lakers stung, the Clippers had made the play-offs for the first time in six years. They had repaid their fans' faith with a winning season and earned a matchup against the Memphis Grizzlies in a best-of-seven playoff series.

The Grizzlies were a tough draw for the Clippers. Like the Clippers, Memphis had a few young and talented players, a few proven veterans, and a deep bench. Center Marc Gasol, as well as forwards Rudy Gay and Zach Randolph (a former Clipper), made up a strong core for Memphis that would push the Clippers to their limits. Blake and the Clippers crew couldn't afford to fall behind in the series. They needed to win game one and take the momentum from the Grizzlies.

But the Clippers started the game flat. The Grizzlies outscored them thirty-four to sixteen in the first quarter, and with two minutes left in the third quarter, Lob City was down by twenty-seven points, with the score 84–57 in favor of Memphis. Clippers fans were shaking their heads. The franchise really did seem to be cursed.

Except, that night, the Clippers finally broke the curse with a fourth-quarter performance that shocked the entire league, unleashing an offensive onslaught that the Grizzlies could not match. In the last minutes of the third and through the whole fourth quarter, the Clippers had a 26–1 run and outscored the Grizzlies, 42–14. They did it from all over the court, too. Guard Nick Young shot three three-pointers, Blake hit from the post, and Mo Williams hit from all over the court, while Chris Paul dropped in some signature twenty-footers. The team was unstoppable. Chris hit clutch free throws with twenty-three seconds left to put the Clippers on top for the first time in that game. After trailing since the tip, the Clippers battled back to win, 99–98. "I don't think I've been part of a game like that ever," Blake said. "It was unbelievable."

It was one of the greatest comebacks in the franchise's history—and in NBA playoff history as well. That win changed the mentality of the team, and it proved to the fans and the league that the Clippers were a fighting team that would be tough to take down. They were going to scrap and fight for every ball and every point until the final whistle.

That game turned out to be the first of a very

physical series. It was a back-and-forth affair, and in the end, the Clippers lost game two with a score of 105–98, but they had done what they set out to do in Memphis. They had split the first two games and were headed home with the series tied.

Game three followed a familiar pattern. The Clippers were down early and trailed for most of the second half. As they had all season, the Clippers' two stars led the team back into the game.

Blake and Chris had developed good nonverbal communication during that season, and it was put on display late in game three. As Chris Paul drove to the basket, the Grizzlies' two big men collapsed in the paint to deny him the lane. Chris feathered a bounce pass softly into Blake's hands as the power forward ran the baseline. Blake crushed the ball home. It was one of those great plays that had everyone, including coaches and players, shaking their heads in disbelief.

The Clippers were becoming a team that was as mentally tough as they were physically tough. They believed they were capable of winning every game, and that made them dangerous. With that win, the Clippers were well on their way to eliminating Memphis from the playoffs.

After another tight win in game four, the Clippers were exhausted—and it showed. Game five was their toughest test. Memphis had turned up the physicality in that game, with Marc Gasol and Zach Randolph banging bodies down low and grinding out every point. The Clippers lost the lead in the first quarter and could not mount a big enough comeback that game. They were simply too worn down. Still, the Grizzlies would have to win the last two games to take the series. The Clippers needed to win only one.

They hoped that game six would be the final game. Blake's knee was bothering him, and he needed a game-time decision to determine whether he was healthy enough to play. In the end, he decided to play—even though he wasn't at his best. The Clippers led by eight in the fourth quarter, but this time it was Memphis who mounted an improbable comeback to win by two. It was a heartbreaker. Blake had done his best, but his seventeen points weren't enough to make up for the lack of output from Chris, who scored only eleven. Blake also pulled in an uncharacteristically low five rebounds that game. Memphis's post players were getting a position on him because of the knee injury. If the

Clippers were going to advance, they would need more from a healthy Blake.

It all came down to game seven. The winner would go on to face the incredibly talented San Antonio Spurs, who had swept the Utah Jazz, and the losing team would have to start the off-season.

Every time the Clippers took the lead, the Grizzlies stole it back. Blake looked worse than he had during game six, and while he had the elevation, he couldn't pivot on his left knee, which prevented him from making post moves to the right. The Grizzlies knew that he had to go left with the ball, which made him predictable and easy to defend. It also made it easier for Memphis to box out Blake.

Chris Paul took the weight of the team on his shoulders and kept them in the game until the fourth quarter, when the Los Angeles bench stepped up and took over. Mo Williams, Nick Young, and Kenyon Martin all made big plays off the bench for the Clippers. Chris Paul had nineteen points, while Nick dropped thirteen, and Kenyon added eleven. The Clippers won the game 82–72 to take the series and advance to the Western Conference semifinals!

It was the Clippers' third playoff series win in

forty-one years, and Los Angeles was falling in love with the team. They had a strong work ethic and will to win that endeared them to practically every basketball fan in Southern California.

But the next series was against the Spurs, and the Spurs hadn't lost a game in over a month. On top of that, they had been resting while Blake, Chris, and the Clippers were battling the Grizzlies for seven tough games.

Blake's knee wasn't necessarily getting worse, but it wasn't getting better with rest, either. If this were the regular season, he wouldn't have been able to play for at least two weeks. However, the Clippers didn't have two weeks. He would have to play—but could he play well?

The Spurs had future Hall-of-Famer Tim Duncan manning the paint while guards Tony Parker, Danny Green, and Manu Ginóbili made up a formidable backcourt rotation. The real strength of the team, however, was the depth of the Spurs' bench. They had players on the bench who were good enough to be starters on most other NBA teams.

The Clippers limped into the series and lost both games in San Antonio before heading back to Los Angeles. Down 2–0, the Clippers tried to whip up a fight at home for the fans, but the Spurs were tough that season. Even when the Clippers took a lead, the Spurs would chip away at it, never panicked or worried. They just wore the Clippers down and ended each game with the win. Ultimately, the Spurs swept the Clippers and moved on to the Western Conference finals against the Oklahoma City Thunder.

The series loss was not the way the Clippers had wanted to end the season. Still, everyone knew that it had been a historic one for the franchise, with Blake and Chris as one of the best frontcourt-backcourt duos in the NBA that year. The Clippers could hold their heads high.

For the first time in years, everyone was talking about what the Clippers were going to do in the off-season. There weren't any glaring holes on the team—they just needed to upgrade at a few positions and add bench depth. With the right pieces, the Clippers could be real contenders. The hope of the last off-season had turned into excitement and expectation. The energy around the team was electric.

CHAPTER ELEVEN
2012–2013

BUILDING A CHAMPION IS NEVER EASY

The Clippers front office was very busy during the 2012 off-season. Owner Donald Sterling curiously allowed general manager Neil Olshey to bolt for Portland before promoting the unknown Gary Sacks from inside the front office. Gary would work with Coach Del Negro to come up with the off-season plan.

The first agenda item on the team's list was to re-sign some of their talent. The Clippers signed Blake to a five-year contract worth up to $95 million, then signed Chauncey Billups to a new one-year deal. The next item on the Clippers' off-season checklist was to upgrade several positions. The Clippers let Randy Foye and Nick Young walk in free agency and signed former Portland Trail Blazer Jamal Crawford to a four-year, $21 million contract. They then traded Mo Williams to Utah and the rights to Furkan Aldemir to Houston for former Laker Lamar Odom.

Lastly, the front office signed Grant Hill and Matt Barnes as veteran presences on the team. In his prime, Grant Hill had been one of the best players in the league, and he had been through every possible scenario. Now forty years old, he would provide great locker room leadership and could help the second unit keep its composure in big games. Matt Barnes had been with the Lakers the season before and could do whatever was asked of him efficiently.

Once everything was in place, it was time to see how the pieces, old and new, worked together. Expectations were high. Was the Clippers team good enough to contend in the playoffs once again? This team was built to win now, but these players had not been through any games together. If the chemistry wasn't there, the Clippers might be doomed to slide right back toward so-so play. Missing the playoffs was not an option if they were going to convince everyone that they were contenders, not pretenders.

The Clippers opened their season against the Memphis Grizzlies, and the new Clippers lineup clearly worked better than when the two teams had met in the playoffs. The main difference was the Clippers bench. Jamal Crawford, Eric Bledsoe, Lamar Odom, and Ronny Turiaf made for a formidable second unit. The Grizzlies couldn't keep up with the Clippers' depth, especially with Jamal Crawford dropping twenty-nine points off the bench. Six Clippers scored in double figures, and everyone who played scored at least one basket.

That season was defined by the Clippers' winning and losing streaks. They started 2–2 before going on a six-game winning streak. They followed that up with a four-game losing streak, before doing something the franchise had never done before. Sitting at 8–6 and looking like a solid team, the Clippers decided to stop losing.

They won four, then six, then twelve, then seventeen games in a row. This was during the heart of their schedule, with some of their toughest games. They beat playoff teams and cellar dwellers alike, on the road and at home.

"It's a tribute to everybody in here," Blake said. "Everybody has been a huge part one night or the other. It's a selfless attitude the team has taken on. This is the most fun I've ever had playing basketball."

During the magnificent run, the Clippers won

eleven of the seventeen games by twelve or more points. Their second unit had been playing so well that Chris and Blake didn't need to play during the final quarter of many games. By the time the streak ended, the Clippers had the best road record in the league and the best overall record in the league. They were firing on all cylinders.

The All-Star Game was good to the Clippers, too.

Andrew D. Bernstein/Getty Images

BLAKE DUNKS AGAINST THE LOS ANGELES LAKERS IN 2012.

Both Blake and Chris Paul started for the West, and just seconds into the game, Chris Paul hit Blake for a great dunk. That night, Chris and Blake led the West to a 143–138 victory. Blake put up nineteen points, three rebounds, three assists, and two steals, while Chris was named the All-Star Game MVP for his twenty points, fifteen assists, and four steals.

After the Denver Nuggets finally snapped the Clippers' winning streak, the Clippers were able to focus on the rest of the season and prepare for the playoffs. They ended the season with another streak, winning their last seven games before heading into the postseason as the fourth seed. The Clippers would have to face the Memphis Grizzlies again.

The Grizzlies went into the playoffs confident. They were playing their best basketball of the season and had peaked at the right time. Somebody would have to body up the strong Memphis frontcourt to keep the Clippers close, but Blake was not the player for the job the first game. He surprised the fans at the Staples Center by missing dunks and getting into early foul trouble that limited his game time. He seemed to be too amped up for the game and was making silly mistakes. Overall, he had a weak performance by his own standards.

Fortunately, the rest of the team stepped up. Eleven different players snagged rebounds to help the Clippers keep pace with Memphis, and Chris Paul led the team in scoring with twenty-three points, while seven players scored in double figures. In a total team effort, the Clippers cruised to a 112–91 win.

Blake was completely focused in game two. He wanted to atone for his poor performance in game one, and he was calmer and more directed. He scored thirteen points in the first quarter alone and flexed some serious muscle under the basket. Blake found his dunk again that night. Every dunk got the crowd fired up.

For a stretch in the second quarter, no one could stop Jamal Crawford, either. The Grizzlies tried to to use multiple players on him, but Jamal hit from everywhere on the court. On one play, he dribbled through two defenders, then pulled up to hit a twelve-footer with three hands in his face!

The Clippers sat on a twelve-point lead at one point, but they started to cool in the third quarter and let the Grizzlies chip away at the lead. Luckily, the Clippers had a player on the team who could make a clutch shot with an army of defenders in his face: Chris Paul, who proved his worth again. The Grizzlies tied the game with just over five seconds left and were expecting to take the game into extra time. That's when Chris got the ball.

Just inside half-court, Chris started to drive to the basket, then dragged his feet to slow down before he drove to the basket again. The speed change forced the defenders to play catch-up, giving Chris just enough space to glide down the edge of the paint and float the ball through the basket as time ended.

Blake was the first to hug the point guard and celebrate the 93–91 win. Chris's twenty-four points, along with Blake's twenty-one, were enough to give the Clippers a two-game lead before heading to Memphis. The Clippers had the momentum—they only needed to win two of the next five games, while the Grizzlies needed to win four. Everything was in the Clippers' favor.

For everything that the Clippers achieved that season, for all the streaks and all their wins, what happened next reminded fans that this team had been cursed for most of its history. Everything went wrong from that moment: Blake sprained an ankle, Chris got thrown out of game six—nothing went the

Clippers' way. It was as if the Clippers were destined to fail. The expectation for that season had swelled in the fans' hearts until their hope was higher than it had been in years, but that series against the Grizzlies slammed Clippers fans back down to earth.

The Grizzlies won four games in a row to take the series, and they headed to the conference semifinals for the second time in three years. It was a collapse of epic proportions. This Clippers culture of losing would have to change.

CHAPTER TWELVE
2013–2014

THE NEXT LEVEL

It wasn't the fact that the Clippers couldn't get past Memphis in the playoffs—it was the way the team had collapsed that was a cause for concern. It had been such a historic season for the franchise, its best ever. But then the Clippers had lost four straight playoff games to crash out of the postseason.

Coach Del Negro's inability to make the necessary adjustments to compete during the last four games of the playoffs ended his chances of being offered a contract extension. The Clippers' priority was to re-sign Chris Paul to a multiyear extension, but the star point guard wanted to know whom he'd playing for, so the Clippers focused on securing a coach first.

The front office and ownership looked at all the big names available that summer. When rumors of trouble between the Boston Celtics and their decorated head coach, Doc Rivers, began to surface, the Clippers saw an opportunity. Before formally asking the Celtics for permission to meet with Rivers, the Clippers decided to reach out to him through back channels to check his interest. Coach Rivers made it known that he was very interested, but only if he and Boston were moving on from each other. He had coached the Celtics for nine years and brought Boston the 2008 NBA Championship, its first since 1988, and—this was the main issue—he was still under contract. The Clippers would need to trade with the Celtics, and after a tense negotiating period, the Clippers sent their 2015 first-round draft pick to Boston in exchange for the final three years of Doc Rivers's coaching contract.

Coach Rivers's signature on a contract set in motion a series of quick roster moves that made the Clippers the biggest off-season players that year. First, Coach Rivers's championship pedigree enticed Chris Paul into signing a five-year, $107 million contract. With Chris Paul on the books, Coach Rivers had Blake, Chris, DeAndre Jordan, and Jamal Crawford all signed to multiyear contracts. The Clippers' core was intact.

Then, Coach Rivers needed to add to his bench. By the end of the previous season, the bench had been tired, and teams had figured out how to wear down the Clippers throughout a game. In a great move for the team, the Clippers traded Eric Bledsoe and Caron Butler to the Phoenix Suns and got forward Jared Dudley from Phoenix and former AP Player of the Year J.J. Redick from Milwaukee in a three-team trade. Gone that season were Grant Hill, Chauncey Billups, and Ronny Turiaf. On paper, the Clippers team looked stronger than last year, but the Memphis series had proved that looks could be deceiving.

Coach Rivers had a big job ahead. He needed to bring a winning culture to a franchise known for losing and also make DeAndre Jordan into the defensive force under the net that he had the potential to be.

The head coach also needed to build balance on offense. During the previous season, the Clippers ran the pick and roll with a lot of success, but teams had begun to figure out how to shut that offensive strategy down. Coach Rivers needed to get Blake and the rest of the team more involved.

During the first two years of his career, Blake had gained a reputation for being soft because he was a nice guy and wasn't as aggressive as some of the other players. Even though he wasn't soft by any means, many in the media and even some players took to saying that Blake was exactly that, letting the label take a life of its own.

Jeff Gross/Getty Images Sport

BLAKE AND HIS TEAMMATES J.J. REDICK (#4), CHRIS PAUL (#3), DEANDRE JORDAN (#6), AND MATT BARNES (#22) POSE WITH COACH DOC RIVERS IN 2014.

To fight against the label, Blake had spent that off-season working on a new array of offensive moves and increasing his fitness levels. People said that all he could do was dunk and that he could dunk from anywhere on the floor. Throughout his career Blake had been an awesome player above the rim. He could always jump high, but that off-season he had further developed his post moves with both hands going both directions, while perfecting a consistent midrange jumper and improving his free throw shooting. With his improved play came an increase in confidence. He felt stronger, he acted stronger, and he made decisions more quickly.

Doc Rivers had also worked his magic on Blake, transforming him into a defensive force. This season would change everyone's impression of him. Nobody would call him soft again.

By the start of the season, Doc Rivers's new philosophies had taken root within the team, but those ideas did not find their way onto the court right away. It would take time to incorporate the new defensive schemes and set plays on offense. The Clippers lost to the Lakers in the first game of the season before beating the Golden State Warriors, Sacramento Kings, and Houston Rockets. During each of the first four games, the offense broke the 100-point mark, maxing out at 137 points against the Rockets. But they also let the opposing teams score over 100 points. The offense was clicking, and it would be one of the best in the league by the end of the season—but the defense was a work in progress. It wasn't until game fifteen that the team adopted the defensive toughness Coach Rivers wanted to see. From that game on, eleven of the next fourteen games had the Clippers holding their opponents to under 100 points, and they won ten of those games.

By late December, the Clippers had won twenty games and lost nine. Blake had found his double-double rhythm with seventeen double-doubles, and was averaging 18.2 points and 9.5 rebounds. Chris Paul led the team the rest of the way.

On Christmas Day, the Clippers played their fiercest rivals outside of Los Angeles, the Golden State Warriors. At the end of the third quarter, small forward Draymond Green was ejected for elbowing Blake in an off-the-ball foul. The referees gave Blake a technical for yelling at Green after the play, and Blake was clearly upset.

The Warriors frontcourt was playing much too physically that night, elbowing, pushing, and grabbing Blake's jersey. Not long after the technical, Blake and Warriors center Andrew Bogut got tangled up, and another scuffle broke out. Bogut and Blake both got technical fouls, which meant Blake was headed to the locker room with almost all of the fourth quarter remaining.

Even though he left the game early, Blake still totaled twenty points and fourteen rebounds. Chris, the team leader after Blake was ejected, had a game-high twenty-six points and eleven assists, but after blowing a thirteen-point lead and being down 105–103, Chris was swatted trying to tie the game with seconds on the clock. The Clippers lost.

Over Blake's career, there were moments or games that he would use as motivation. Those games would push him to get better. The game against the Warriors was one of those. It lit a fire in Blake, and even though the league had later admitted that he should not have been given the second technical or ejected, that game was burned into his mind. From that point on, he was determined to match the physical play of any team.

He had monster performances in two of his next four games, leading the Clippers over the Utah Jazz with forty points, ten rebounds, three assists, a steal, and a block and then dropping thirty-one points, twelve rebounds, and two assists on the Charlotte Bobcats two games later.

All of Blake's extra off-season work was paying off. Blake carried the team when Chris Paul went down with a nasty shoulder injury in early January that kept him out of nineteen games and when J.J. Redick was lost for twenty-five games after hurting his back a month later. By midseason, the league was talking about Blake as a potential MVP candidate, and he had the Clippers vying for the top spot in the West. He was voted to his fourth consecutive All-Star Game and was tapped to start alongside such players as Steph Curry, Kevin Durant, and Kevin Love.

That year, the NBA All-Star Game was in New Orleans. During the game, the league's leading scorer, Kevin Durant, and Blake put on a show for the fans. Blake spent the game doing exactly what everyone criticized him for: he dunked the ball—a lot. He did two-handed power slams, soaring tomahawks from the top of the key, spinning post moves that ended with thunderous, rim-hanging jams, windmills, alley-oops, and high-flying put-backs. It was a slam-dunk spectacular.

In the end, he didn't need to prove anything to anyone by showing off his "new game." He was simply taking great shots, and he was going to give the fans what they wanted. Blake scored eighteen of his twenty first-half points in the first quarter alone. Blake and Durant both scored thirty-eight points that game, which was good enough for the third highest total in an All-Star Game behind only Wilt Chamberlain (forty-two) and Michael Jordan (forty). Blake's nineteen-of-twenty-three shooting set a record for field goals made in an All-Star Game. Despite their best efforts, the West lost to the East in a high-scoring affair of 163–155.

After the All-Star break, the Clippers put together an eleven-game winning streak, during which Blake led the team with an average of 23.8 points per game,

13 rebounds, and 4.5 assists. Blake won his first NBA Player of the Month award and was in the top five for the MVP. Blake finished the season with forty-three double-doubles and multiple career-high averages. His 24.1 points, 9.5 rebounds, and 3.8 assists during the regular season were good enough for third in MVP balloting, behind only Kevin Durant and LeBron James. Blake was *that* good.

The Clippers won twenty of their last twenty-five games and finished the season with fifty-seven wins, the third-best record in the league, behind the Thunder, earning them a third seed in the West. Of course, that position also meant a heated playoff series, this time with the Golden State Warriors.

Blake hadn't cared much for the Warriors since he had been wrongly ejected in the last game against the Northern California team. Some would say that the Warriors played the game as it was meant to be played: tough and physical. Others would say they played dirty. It is a fine line between the two opinions, and the Warriors walked right on it.

After the heated games that season, this was exactly what each team wanted—a chance to knock the other out of the playoffs. There is nothing better than ending your rival's season while you still get to play. "You know what it is? They want to beat us, and we want to beat them," Coach Rivers said. "We're in their way, and they're in our way, and somebody has got to get out of the way."

The Warriors were missing some key pieces as they headed into the playoffs. Andrew Bogut, their center, had an injury that would keep him out of the series with the Clippers. This would free up Blake inside and help the Clippers focus their defensive energies on a Warriors backcourt that contained Stephen Curry and Klay Thompson.

In game one, Klay Thompson did his thing early and put the Clippers on their heels. Blake had a disappointing game, however, and by early in the second quarter, he was in severe foul trouble after Marreese Speights took a charge. Blake was called for his third foul, forcing him to ride the bench for the rest of the half. In the end, Blake's sixteen points and three rebounds did not match up with Klay Thompson's twenty-two points, seven rebounds, and five assists, and the Warriors took the game by a score of 109–105.

"We made mistakes," Blake said. "Some of us, myself included, maybe wanted it too much and came in with an expectation. We just need to relax."

It was time to play Clippers ball, or the season

would be over before they knew it. That meant coming out hard and fast, taking it to the Warriors from the start of the game. They couldn't afford to lose the first two games at home before going on the road to Oakland. That meant an aggressive, physical game—Blake's favorite type.

Blake had a terrific game and stayed out of foul trouble—a single foul wasn't called on him all night. With fourteen points in the first quarter, he showed the Warriors what to expect early. He was still working his slam dunks, but it was his heads-up play that made the difference. He found a way to outrun everyone on the court and scored multiple buckets. He also took advantage of the small lineup the Warriors were using—unsuccessfully—to stretch the court. Midway through the second quarter, the Clippers were up twenty, and they cruised the rest of the game. Blake dropped thirty-five points, on thirteen-of-seventeen shooting. It was a 138–98 blowout.

Tied at one game apiece and headed to Oakland to play the Warriors on the road, the Clippers had only one thought on their minds: they had to get a road win. If the Clippers believed that game three would be another blowout, they were wrong. Blake again led the team in points with thirty-two, but the teammate who made a big difference was DeAndre Jordan. His fourteen points and twenty-two rebounds, fifteen of which were defensive, changed the game. DeAndre was on every bad shot and grabbed every ball that bounced off the rim. Each defensive rebound kept the Warriors from a second-chance basket.

Chris Paul had fifteen points and defended Steph Curry all night. At the end of the game, Chris forced a bad three-point shot from the Warriors point guard as time expired, and the Clippers squeaked by with a nail-biting 98–96 win.

Then came the off-the-court distractions.

Donald Sterling, the Clippers owner who had consistently been in trouble with the league, was recorded making derogatory remarks about African American basketball players. That recording was made back in September 2013 by a friend, Ms. Stiviano, and though she made the Clippers front office aware of the recording on April 9, 2014, they sat on the information for most of the month. In the recording, Donald Sterling could be heard asking Ms. Stiviano not to bring African Americans with her to Clippers games and telling her that he did not want her associating with black people at all, among other statements.

It was terrible behavior. The league—and the

nation—had come far from prejudice and oppression against people of color, but this recording was a reminder that racism was still a huge problem in sports and in everyday life across America. This hateful behavior could not be allowed to stand.

The recording was leaked to the media on April 25, the day after the Clippers' game three win. The news rocked the Clippers to their foundation, along with the NBA and all of basketball. The NBA vowed to investigate the validity of the recording, but the players knew they had to do something on the court to make a statement.

"I think the biggest statement we can make as men—not as black men, as men—is to stick together and show how strong we are as a group, not splinter, not walk," said Coach Rivers.

Three days later, the Warriors tied up the series in a twenty-one-point blowout of their own. They came out aggressively, while the Clippers looked heavy and sluggish. The scandal had worn on the players. It was like a weight around their necks.

Steph Curry went off for thirty-three points, seven assists, and seven rebounds that night, but the real news was what happened during the pregame shootaround. It was a subtle statement, a simple gesture, but it spoke volumes.

When the Clippers players came out of the locker room, they took their warm-ups off at center court, dropped them on the Golden State Warriors logo, and revealed that their red team shirts had been turned inside out to hide the team logo and name. That night, the players weren't playing for the team: they were playing for themselves, for one another, and for respect and justice for people of color. They had never played for the team's owner, and they weren't going to ignore his actions any longer.

Everyone was asking about Donald Sterling's comments and had looked past the basketball that was still to be played. It made it hard to play the game when something so serious and important was happening all around them.

"There's not a team that has gone through this," Blake said. "I remember Saturday morning, when everything had hit, you could see certain players that were really [emotional] about the situation. This was the first day, and it got bigger. At the point when we had the meeting, it was a huge thing, but it just grew and grew and grew with each day and each hour, honestly, and it just wore on guys. We tried to put it off to the side, but it's impossible."

The Clippers lost big that night, but nobody held it against them. They had gone through so much. Besides, the series was only tied 2–2, and anything was possible. The Clippers would need to regroup before game five.

Between games, sponsors began to withdraw their endorsements of the Clippers. The National Association for the Advancement of Colored People (NAACP) had been just about to give Donald Sterling a lifetime achievement award and immediately withdrew it. The public outcry was deafening. The fans and the media had had enough. It was time for Donald Sterling to go.

April 29, 2014, was an emotional and exhausting day. Before the game, NBA commissioner Adam Silver held a press conference to announce Donald Sterling's fate in the NBA. His penalties were swift and decisive. Racism and racist behavior would not be tolerated anywhere in the NBA. Commissioner Silver banned Donald Sterling from the NBA for life, fined him $2.5 million (the maximum allowed), and announced plans to force a sale of the Clippers to new owners, effectively ending Sterling's involvement in the NBA and basketball.

Later that night, the Clippers returned to Los Angeles to play game five, unsure what the atmosphere would be like. They soon found that the fans supported the team and racial equality above anything else. During the game, the capacity crowd at the Staples Center started to chant "We are one" over and over and over. Others, both inside and outside the stadium, held signs that read HATE WILL NEVER WIN and RISE ABOVE and NO TIME FOR RACISM. It was a magical moment for the players and for basketball. The commissioner's decision meant a lot to the team, and it felt like some justice had been delivered.

With the fans behind them and the momentum of the series on the line, the Clippers put together a total team effort. Six players scored in the double digits, and four scored over twenty points. Blake and Chris led the team with twenty-four points and twenty-two points, respectively, while DeAndre Jordan pulled in eighteen rebounds and added three blocks. The Clippers beat the Warriors, 113–103.

The Warriors won game six to force a series-deciding seventh match. The Clippers fans deserved a win. Los Angeles deserved a win. But above all, the players deserved it. They had been through more than any other team in the NBA had gone through in decades, if not ever, and they had remained strong in the face of enormous emotional pressure. They had stood for racial equality and had endured countless questions—and in the end, they'd played their games as best they could. Each night, they gave it all they had, and though they didn't win every game, they won enough to force game seven. They needed one more.

Blake got rolling from the tip. He had nine by the second quarter, but still Golden State was leading early. The Clippers were doing everything they could, but they just couldn't catch the Warriors. It wasn't until late in the third quarter, when the Clippers outscored the Warriors 31–20, that the Clippers took their first lead of the game on a J.J. Redick bucket. The Clippers were 34–0 when leading after three quarters, so they knew how to close out a game.

On one play midway through the fourth, Blake reeled in a Steph Curry turnover and barreled through Draymond Green to lay the ball in. Minutes later, DeAndre Jordan swatted the ball from Steph, before J.J. Redick pushed the ball upcourt and alley-ooped Blake, who crushed the ball home. The best play of the night was when Blake spun toward the baseline from the top of the paint and drove at the hoop, twisted to avoid the defender, and threw the ball up with his back to the basket before crashing to the ground and rolling head over heels while the ball went through the iron. It was as acrobatic a play as any seen all year.

The Clippers were sent to the line down the stretch and hit their free throws, sealing the game—they'd held on for the win and were headed to the conference semifinals for the second time in three years. Everyone was fired up, but the players were exhausted. It was a historic win for the franchise, and the only problem now was that the Clippers would have to face the best team of the regular season: the Oklahoma City Thunder. It seemed like basketball always came back to Oklahoma for Blake.

The Thunder and the Clippers were two high-octane offensive teams. The Thunder had the regular season scoring champ in Kevin Durant, but the Clippers were the highest-scoring team, with an average of 107.9 points per game. Blake and Chris Paul could match up with any team in the league, and the Clippers would need some other players to step up as well. They would also need Chris Paul to be 100 percent healthy; he had been nursing an aching hamstring through the last series, and he'd need to rest.

Lastly, Blake would need to find a way to win the battle with the Thunder's Serge Ibaka. Blake and

Serge Ibaka had a history of intense games. Over the last three years, the two had gotten into some epic physical battles that harked back to the early days of the NBA. Serge had proven to be one of Blake's toughest matchups and a defensive nightmare for him, ever since coming into the league from Spanish team Ricoh Manresa. Serge had twice been the NBA blocks leader and had been named to NBA All-Defensive First Team for the last three seasons. The competition between the two was going to be fierce.

Game one went the Clippers' way. Chris Paul was on fire with eight three-pointers, scoring thirty-two points on twelve of fourteen shots and dishing ten assists. The Clippers set the tone early, forcing turnovers and executing their game plan, despite being out-rebounded 31–47. Blake put in a solid shift with twenty-three points, five rebounds, and five assists. It was a strong start to the series for the Clippers, who were looking to advance to the conference finals for the first time in franchise history. And, more important, the Clippers had stolen a game on the road. It was exactly how they wanted to start the series.

The Clippers lost game two by eleven points and returned home to the rabid Clippers fans in L.A. with the series tied up. They lost game three as

Thunder point guard Russell Westbrook and Kevin Durant scored fifty-nine points together. After being up 1–0 in the series, the Clippers now found themselves down 2–1. They needed to make some adjustments, and right away, before the series slipped out of their grasp. The problem was that the Oklahoma City Thunder team had simply been outplaying the Clippers for most of the last two games. The Clippers were losing the battle inside and had been outrebounded in every game in the series. It wasn't their offense that was the problem—it was that the Clippers had to find a way to stop the Thunder's offensive machine. It was chewing them up.

Game four was a must-win for the Clippers. After all the turmoil from the Warriors series, they couldn't risk going down two games.

The Thunder jumped out to an early lead and outplayed the Clippers for most of three quarters. Late in the game and down 75–63, something came alive in the Clippers. Blake, who had twenty-five points, and Chris, who had twenty-three points and ten assists, were doing their best to keep pace with the Thunders, but Kevin Durant was lights out that night, and the Clippers' outside shooting had completely dried up. The Clippers had only made three three-pointers out of twenty-one shots beyond the arc that night. When things go wrong for a team, it often takes a special effort from the most unlikely of places. That night, it was backup point guard Darren Collison who stepped up. He scored ten of the Clippers' last twenty points to complete a comeback that tied up the series 2–2 with a 101–99 win. The Clippers had a knack for making comebacks from double-digit deficits—this was their fourteenth that season. A big part of the comeback was the team's ability to limit the Thunder's second chances.

Propped up by their comeback in game four, the Clippers roared out of the tunnel and scrapped for every point as game five started. The Clippers were up as many as fifteen points in the first quarter, but the Thunder clawed their way back into the game to take a one-point lead in the second. The Clippers had led for the entire game, until the Thunder gave them a taste of their own medicine. At the end, with just seconds on the clock, Chris Paul made a bad pass that was picked off by Russell Westbrook, then fouled the Thunder's point guard as he was trying to shoot a three-pointer. Westbrook hit all three foul shots, and the Thunder stole the game. The Clippers were almost completely deflated.

Blake still had some fight in him, however. The next game would be in Los Angeles, and the fans would bring their energy, too, which should help, but the Clippers would need more from Blake and Chris to force a game seven. The Clippers began with a hot start, taking the quick lead, and were looking to extend it into double digits when Kevin Durant scored nine points in seventy-seven seconds on back-to-back-to-back three-pointers. Every time Blake dunked the ball or Chris Paul hit a jumper, Kevin Durant did something to keep the Thunder in the game. He was everywhere. If the Clippers pulled ahead, the Thunder tightened the score back up again. It was frustrating for the Clippers to gain the smallest amount of momentum, just to have it crushed by an Oklahoma City surge.

It was even worse when it seemed like the Thunder players were getting all the referees' favorable calls, and it drained the Clippers' spirits. Blake was called for two questionable fouls late in the fourth and was out of the game. That left the Clippers with a big hole in the lineup. From the start, the two teams had been closely matched, but the Thunder had a slight advantage. With Blake out, the Thunder had a much bigger advantage. The Clippers fought and scrapped to the very last, but in the end, the Thunder bounced them from the playoffs and ended their season.

It had been a confusing season full of franchise

firsts. On one hand, the team had won more games in a single season than any Clippers team in franchise history, and yet they still hadn't found a way to make it to the conference finals.

While the Clippers came up short of their goal to be world champions, Blake's arrival had set in motion a series of events that ultimately led to changes that shook the franchise out of its long slumber and awakened a real title contender. Jamal Crawford had benefited from Blake's game that season, and he was named NBA Sixth Man of the Year for best bench player in the league. Chris, Blake, and DeAndre formed the core of a talented roster, and the more they played together, the more they improved.

"A lot of stuff went wrong for us throughout this, and we just kept going," Coach Rivers said about the season. "So, that's the lesson for us. You have to embrace how hard it is. You have to actually enjoy how hard it is. And whoever wins it is going to say that.

"I thought that was growth for us at least. I think they understood. I don't know if we got that until the playoffs started," continued Coach Rivers. "That's why… I told the guys before, 'You grow during the playoffs. Don't think you don't grow and come together.'"

They had grown. They had grown closer to each

other after going through the off-court distractions, battling on the court together, and supporting each other through loss. They had grown into Coach Rivers's basketball talents. They had grown into a family.

Blake had also grown that year. He had always been a leader with his play, but that year he became a leader off the court, too. He had always been charitable, having previously announced that he would donate $100 for every dunk he performs in a game to the Dunking for Dollars campaign to fight childhood obesity. His on-court leadership was dynamic, showcasing an array of offensive moves that made him a strong player around the basket. His locker-room presence and jokes kept everyone loose, while his perseverance on the court helped the team come back in more than a dozen games that season. He worked tirelessly to be the best he could be. He chased every ball, even if that meant flying into the crowd. He had given everything he had, and he had left it all on the court during the game six loss to the Thunder. So, when the Clippers lost, it shattered Blake. It crushed the whole team.

No one will know what happened in the locker room after that loss, but the team was clearly emotional. It had been a tough season, with so many obstacles, and now suddenly it was over.

CHAPTER THIRTEEN
2014 AND BEYOND

THE DAWN OF A NEW ERA

When the Clippers lost to the Thunder in game six, the players' season was over, but for the Clippers front office, it had just begun. In the weeks following the loss, the NBA worked on facilitating the sale of the team. Initially, Donald Sterling fought the league and tried to stop the sale, but by the end of the summer, he and his wife, Shelly, had sold the Clippers to former Microsoft CEO Steve Ballmer for $2 billion. That was the most exciting change to the team that off-season, for both the players and the fans. Ballmer was thrilled to own the team and was ready to infuse the franchise with new energy and a stream of money.

"It's very, very exciting. I'm a basketball nut," Ballmer said. "I look forward to supporting the community, the fan base, the staff, Doc [Rivers], and the players to take this thing to higher heights."

The attitude around the team had changed.

There was a new energy. The team was headed in a new direction, but they didn't need to rebuild as much as to reload. Blake was enthusiastic about his team's new owner and about the stability that he would bring to the franchise.

That stability would allow the players to focus on winning and Coach Rivers to focus on getting them ready to compete in every game. The Clippers had gone through an upheaval during the playoffs and had found a way to grind out wins. The team's core—Chris Paul, DeAndre Jordan, and Blake—was healthy, and they now were battle-tested in the postseason. Matt Barnes, Jamal Crawford, and J.J. Redick returned to round out the squad. With a few pieces for depth, this team was built to compete for titles.

And that's exactly what they did, finishing 56–26 for another winning season and securing the third-seed spot in the Western Conference playoffs in one of the best years the Western Conference had ever seen. The Clippers went into the 2015 playoffs strong, beating the San Antonio Spurs, the defending NBA champions, in a grueling seven games of the first round that saw extraordinary play from Blake and his fellow Clippers. It looked like the team would go far—maybe even all the way to the finals—when they were up three games to one in the conference semifinals against the Houston Rockets. But then the Clippers collapsed, losing to the Rockets in the seven-game series. Their season was over.

After that loss, Blake was asked about the Clippers curse. "The Clippers curse when I first got here was number one picks getting hurt [or] not working out; [the team's] draft picks not working out; [and] not making the playoffs [or] not having winning seasons," Blake said. "No one talked about not getting past the second round. Not a single soul talked about that, but now that's what everybody talks about. Just like the last one, we're going to bust through this one."

While the 2014–2015 season ended earlier than Blake and his teammates had hoped, they had come a long way, and they knew that their best days might still be ahead. The season was a good one for Blake, professionally and personally. He had once again been a starter on the All-Star team, and the West won that game, 163–158.

During the postgame press conference following the Clippers' game seven playoff win against the Spurs, Blake brought his infant son, Ford, up to the podium for the first time. Fatherhood was making Blake's life even better, and Blake, Chris Paul, Jamal Crawford, and Matt Barnes would all bring their young kids to their games, giving these basketball-playing fathers more reasons to smile. After all, family and basketball have always been among the most important things in Blake's life.

Even after back-to-back years of tough losses in the semifinals, Blake remains determined to win a championship for the Clippers. He wants to make up for all the losing years. He had already broken the Clippers curse and helped make the team a real contender, and now it was time to bring home some rings. With Blake's game getting better every year and the team stacked with talented players, there is no telling how far they will go. But one thing is certain: Blake will be a key part of his team's successes—by dominating on the court as he has since high school.

Andrew D. Bernstein/National Basketball Association/Getty Images

BLAKE POSES WITH HIS ROOKIE OF THE YEAR AWARD IN 2011.

TURN THE PAGE
FOR MORE
FUN FACTS!

BLAKE GRIFFIN

A DOUBLE-DOUBLE MACHINE

Blake has shot an incredible number of double-doubles, making him one of the most esteemed basketball players in the league. Take a look at his double-double records:

2007–2008
- PPG*: 14.7
- Double-Doubles: 10

2008–2009
- PPG: 22.7
- Double-Doubles: 30

2009–2010
- No Stats—Injury

2010–2011
- PPG: 22.5
- Double-Doubles: 63

2011–2012
- PPG: 20.7
- Double-Doubles: 41

2012–2013
- PPG: 18.0
- Double-Doubles: 41

2013–2014
- PPG: 24.1
- Double-Doubles: 43

* Points per Game

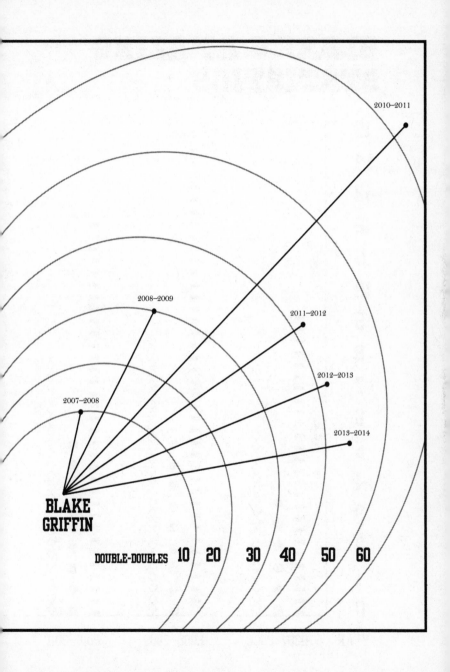

BLAKE'S AMAZING STATISTICS

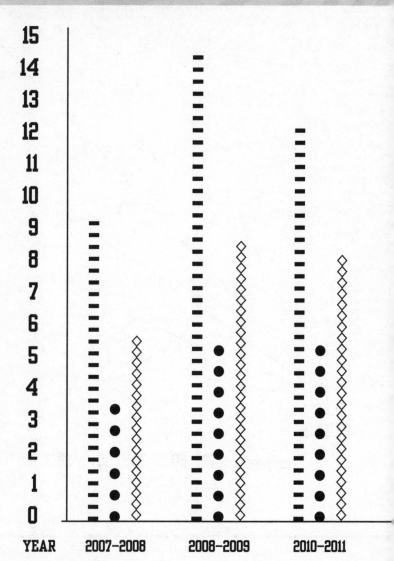

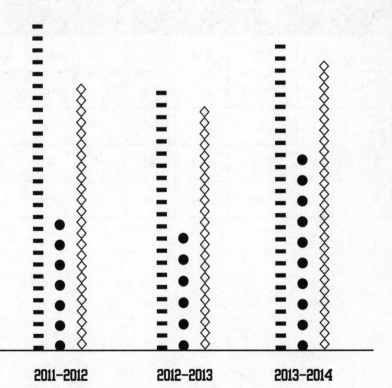

▮ ▮ ▮ ▮ ▮ ▮ REBOUNDS PER GAME
● ● ● ● FREE THROWS MADE PER GAME
◇◇◇◇◇◇ FIELD GOALS MADE PER GAME

* 2009–2010: N/A—INJURY

2011–2012   2012–2013   2013–2014

BLAKE'S NBA CAREER STATISTICS

Year after year, Blake has put up great numbers for his Clippers and All-Star West teams.

REGULAR SEASON

Year	Games	Rebounds	Assists	Steals	Blocks	Points	Average Points per Game
2010–2011	82	989	312	63	45	1845	22.5
2011–2012	66	717	210	54	48	1368	20.7
2012–2013	80	662	299	97	50	1440	18.0
2013–2014	80	757	309	92	51	1930	24.1
2014–2015	67	508	354	63	35	1469	21.9

POSTSEASON

Year	Games	Rebounds	Assists	Steals	Blocks	Points	Average Points per Game
2011–2012	11	76	27	20	10	210	19.1
2012–2013	6	33	15	0	5	79	13.2
2013–2014	13	96	50	16	14	306	23.5
2014–2015	14	178	86	14	14	357	25.5

ALL-STARS

Year	Minutes Played	Rebounds	Assists	Steals	Field Goal Percentages	Points
2010–2011	14:39	5	5	0	66.7%	8
2011–2012	31:26	8	5	2	75%	22
2012–2013	27:24	3	3	2	81.8%	19
2013–2014	31:56	6	1	2	82.6%	38

2014–2015: Blake was once again named as a starter, but had to sit out due to an elbow injury.

GET ON THE FIELD, UNDER THE NET AND BEHIND THE PLATE WITH YOUR
FAVORITE ALL-STARS!

Read the entire Great Americans in Sports series by
MATT CHRISTOPHER